FAST&
LOW

FAST & LOW

Easy Recipes for Low Fat Cuisine

JOAN STILLMAN

Foreword by Sir John Butterfield, M.D.
Regius Professor of Physic, Cambridge University
Chairman, U.K. Medical Research Council and
Agricultural Research Council Nutrition
Committee, 1979–1984

LITTLE, BROWN AND COMPANY
Boston   Toronto

FIRST EDITION

Library of Congress Cataloging in Publication Data
Stillman, Joan, 1917–
 Fast & low.
 Includes index.
 1. Low-fat diet—Recipes. I. Title. II. Title: Fast
and low.
RM237.7.S82   1985   641.5′635   85-5172
ISBN 0-316-81613-2 (pbk.)

Designed by Patricia Girvin Dunbar

FG

Published simultaneously in Canada
by Little, Brown & Company (Canada) Limited

PRINTED IN THE UNITED STATES OF AMERICA

For Bud:
". . . sweet are the uses of adversity"

Acknowledgments

In putting together this collection of recipes, I needed (and got) a lot of help from my friends. Especially I want to thank Corby Kummer for his extraordinary efforts on my behalf; Anne Bernays and Barbara Lawrence, who both gave me a sense of direction; and Gerard Van der Leun, who dreamed up the title. Beth Rashbaum has been a meticulous editor.

Other people were generous with specific ideas about food. I am indebted to Karen Davis, Valerie Brooks, Sybil Hart, Vita Petersen, Leslie Stillman, Anne and Hasan Ozbekhan, Enid Munroe, Didi Lorillard, Martha Hall, Florence Phillips, Patricia Van der Leun, Gloria Watts, and Jozefa Stuart.

David Rush, M.D., Stuart Bartle, M.D., and Barbara Promo, Ph.D., went over the manuscript with professional medical and nutritional expertise and gave me invaluable suggestions.

Bud Stillman is the last man in the world to enjoy any mortification of the flesh. So it was astonishing when, overnight, he gave up all his favorite foods (mainly eggs, steak, and ice cream), and did this without a murmur. Instead, he was endlessly curious and enthusiastic about trying out all the recipes in this book, as they appeared in various forms and at different stages. His suggestions for improvements, for inclusions and deletions, were invaluable. In a sense, we did *Fast and Low* together; certainly it couldn't have been completed without his constant encouragement and marvelous good humor.

Contents

Foreword

by *Sir John Butterfield, M.D.*
Regius Professor of Physic, Cambridge University
Chairman, U.K. Medical Research Council and
Agricultural Research Council Nutrition
Committee, 1979–1984

"A good cook is the best physician," said Andrew Boorde, a physician-monk in the days of Henry VIII. In this book, Joan Stillman is following his observation in two ways: first, by her interest in using herbs in her cooking, and second, by her move toward a low-fat and, therefore, low-calorie diet.

Since the Middle Ages, herbs have been linked to medicinal cures. In this tradition, Joan Stillman's repeated and enthusiastic references to their use to give savor and flavor to her dishes, and her injunctions to grow herbs, reflect the habit of the Middle Ages of cultivating herbs in monastery gardens. These gardens saved the younger monks from going out into the woods looking for herbs whenever they were needed either by the cook or for the care of the sick.

Modern medicine still relies heavily on commercial extensions of these long-standing concepts. Witness the large-scale harvesting of foxgloves for digitalis, used for the treatment of heart disease, as well as the subtle biological engineering employed by pharmaceutical companies in cultivating molds for antibiotics. So our author has one firm link with the history of medicine.

But the other point is her interest in a low-fat diet. This means, automatically, a lower-calorie diet, because fats are so much less rich in calories compared to proteins and carbohydrates. (Each gram of solid fat contains 9 calories, but a gram of lean meat, chicken, or fish contains only 4, as does a gram of carbohydrate.)

The first clear and widely accepted epidemiological evidence of a relationship between diet and disease came in my own field of special interest, diabetes mellitus. In 1870, Bismarck's army besieged Paris, and famine ensued. The Parisian physician Bouchardet observed that his diabetics got better when they lost weight. He also noted, as the famine grew worse, that there were no new cases of diabetes in Paris.

There have been countless confirmations of this important relationship between food intake and diabetic prevalence. During the two world wars in Europe, studies were made of the effects of food restrictions, and other proofs have been offered repeatedly, every time a middle-aged, mildly diabetic patient is helped by a low-calorie dietary regime.

In other fields of human suffering, a major relevant finding came from examinations of the victims of the Nazis. These studies revealed that starvation stripped the fat from the blood vessels of the victims, as well as from their bodies generally. Thus we know that the dreaded deposition of fats (especially cholesterol) in the walls of the arteries of the people of modern civilization, so-called atherosclerosis, is at least in part a reversible condition. I say *in part* because starvation cannot heal scars in blood vessels caused by the irritation that cholesterol creates when it is deposited there. But from this we can conclude that it must be healthier to be slim than to be fat, and that one can win back some lost health, anyway, by dietary means.

With the reestablishment of agriculture in the 1940s and the emergence of thriving postwar economies, together with the sales promotion techniques of supermarkets, the average food consumption in the Western world has soared. Surveys in the United States and in Europe over the past forty years show that our consumption of fats has increased fastest. This is, no doubt, a reflection of the way fats slow down stomach-emptying and so damp down hunger sensations. And most people have just been getting fatter, as is evidenced by the way waist measurements and collar sizes have been gradually rising in all our clothing stores.

Alongside all this, the Western world has suffered an epidemic of heart disease, as well as obesity and diabetes. No one can say exactly what is the cause of any individual's death from heart disease: sometimes the coronary vessel gets thrombosed, sometimes it gets torn during unaccustomed exertion, sometimes there is a hemorrhage into the artery wall that blocks it off. But overall, the epidemic seems to be related to factors in our national life-styles.

Ansel Keys showed long ago that national blood cholesterol levels were closely linked to the frequency of deaths from heart disease recorded country by country. Other investigations have since revealed correlations between heart attacks and many other so-called risk factors — the consumption of saturated (animal) fats or the lack of unsaturated (vegetable) fats in the diet, cigarette smoking, lack of exercise, consumption of alcohol and of coffee, low educational achievements, and so on.

Faced with all this information, authorities concerned with the relationship between national diets and national health in the United States and Europe have been getting together for the past two decades to make recommendations about what the public should be encouraged to eat. In Britain, for example, the Committee on the Medical Aspects of Food Policy, under the chairmanship of the chief medical officer of the Department of Health and, more recently, the National Advisory Committee in Nutrition Education Report, have issued guidelines. In America, the McGovern Report and, in December 1984, the report of the National Institutes of Health came to the same conclusions.

Unanimously, these experts have been saying loudly and clearly that better national health can be achieved by cutting down on fats from meat and dairy products, reducing intakes of salt (to combat high blood pressure in people susceptible to salt-induced hypertension) and of sugar, which in well-fed people is quickly converted to fats — not unexpectedly exactly like those in meat and dairy products! — and, finally, increasing the intake of vegetables and fruits — all rich in fiber.

Readers of what follows in Joan Stillman's book will be interested to see the similarity between all these proposals and exactly what she is recommending in her shopping procedures, her use of the home food processor, and her recipes.

Of course, the complete and sudden introduction of such sweeping changes in national diet away from the products of dairy and cattle farming and toward grain and vegetable consumption would have catastrophic financial consequences for the agricultural and food industries. A joint meeting some years ago of experts from the British Medical Research Council and the British Agricultural and Food Research Council heard estimates ranging into many billions of dollars that would be needed to reorient the food chain and shopping habits of the Western world along the newly proposed lines.

The European Economic Community "butter mountain" and "wine lake" really reflect the systems of food subsidies operating in that economic bloc. Their very size, though, also shows how great will be the economic and political forces that will operate to slow down the rate of major changes in our eating habits.

Much of the material that we read in our newspapers and magazines and see on the television screen can be traced back to the battles going on between different parts of the food industry for their share of the family shopping basket or cart. To some extent, therefore, one must not be surprised if some observers will see Joan Stillman as avant-garde, even slightly revolutionary, in her concepts; for if everyone accepted them overnight, the markets for seeds and for farm equipment, the whole industry of food processing and packaging, the purchasing arrangements of what we eat, et cetera, would be overturned like the moneylenders' tables in the Temple!

Nonetheless, it seems to me inevitable that these changes of diet — toward vegetables and grains and away from meat fats and dairy products — will come about, albeit slowly. This will happen partly through the influence of increasing numbers of "food nuts" on Western food marketplaces, and partly from the worldwide demand for the most highly efficient agricultural–food chain systems possible, in order to prevent food shortages in the face of the rising demands of the world's still-growing total population.

So I am pleased that Joan Stillman has joined the ranks of what I believe is an inevitable march toward healthy eating habits. There seem to be good, solid arguments for her approach and so for this book.

One is brought to this conclusion by considering the relationship between diet and health, by heeding the call of the health promotion folk to reduce our weight to an ideal level and then to maintain it. There can be no doubt that Joan's appetizing, low-fat diet will help us achieve these two worthy objectives.

Her approach is generally in line with the views of international experts on both sides of the Atlantic. What she has worked out and is now advocating may well become general meal-planning in the not too distant future for global as well as for personal reasons.

But perhaps the strongest recommendation I can give for the acquisition of this book for the kitchen shelf is that Joan has shown we don't need to fear the future if, as I believe, this is the way much of the world's consumption is going to have to go. We have nothing to fear, I say, because I can vouch, personally, that Stillman dishes are delicious and Stillman meals are satisfying. The proof, as they say, is in the eating, and there can be absolutely no doubt that Joan Stillman is a good cook and a very strong contender, indeed, for the title of the best physician.

Cambridge, England
February 1985

FAST&
LOW

Introduction

The recent bombshells dropped on the public connecting diet with disease (the report of the National Institutes of Health, December 12, 1984, being the latest) have confirmed what many people have suspected for years. Our national diet, based on animal fats — appearing in red meat, cheese, cream, butter, and egg yolks — contributes to high levels of cholesterol in the blood, and thence to atherosclerosis (sludge in the arteries). Changing over to a regimen of whole grains and beans, fresh fruit and vegetables, chicken, fish, and skim-milk yogurt can sharply reduce cholesterol levels in anyone's blood. A diet like this is now believed to be a good preventive for other diseases, such as diabetes and even cancer.

In our house, we made the switch some five years ago, and like most people, we did it not from choice but from desperation. My husband was suddenly hospitalized with a thrombosis. His cholesterol rate was found to be 380 and his arteries in such terrible shape that he couldn't even qualify for a bypass operation (then thought to be highly desirable).

But the crisis passed, and since there was no alternative, we were urged to try the rigorous Pritikin Program, then being presented in a best-selling book. We studied its pages assiduously, and lived for two months by its rules. The recommended daily two-mile walk turned into a pleasurable habit, but our experience with the food was horrifying. We had never known such sensory deprivation: no fats, sugar, salt, caffeine, or alcohol. I concentrated on the elimination of fats, and cooked with but a drop. It worked. New blood tests showed an improvement that was little short of miraculous. We were nearly bowled over by relief and joy, astounded by the effectiveness of so undramatic a solution.

But how quickly we all adapt. Once survival was more or less assured, we began to groan about the terrible food. I had always been a rather passionate cook, a follower of such gurus as Michael Field, Julia Child, and Elizabeth David. Now their elaborate, fat-filled recipes were not appropriate. So I began searching for diet books. There were hundreds of them, offering lots of nutritional information and dreary recipes. These usually included large sections devoted to — of all things — red meat; the vegetables were usually canned or frozen, the salads inclined toward pineapple and cottage cheese (or worse), and the seasonings were invariably dried: dried garlic, dried parsley, even dried onions.

So, back to *Mastering the Art of French Cooking* and the others, with their truly ingenious combinations and innovative suggestions. I began hacking away at the recipes to get rid of the butter, cream, and eggs. It was nice to find that, even with the fat out, many of the recipes still stood up. I had already discovered this to be true of chicken. Every cookbook in the world tells you to cook these birds in butter or oil. But I found that a roasting chicken is so full of its own fat that it keeps trying to get rid of it throughout the cooking process. The first time I cooked a chicken anointed only with lemon juice, inside and out, it emerged from the oven tender and succulent. As I threw out a panful of grease, I was baffled that I'd spent so many years blindly following tradition.

Still, it's extremely hard to break away from the wisdom of one's elders, and I needed a lot of help in order to do it. At this point I got a number of breaks. First, I bought a Cuisinart food processor, and after circling around it suspiciously for a couple of weeks, began using it and in short order was totally hooked. Second, a number of my friends, thinking along the same lines, started giving me excellent ideas and/or recipes. Third, Asian markets (mostly owned and operated by Koreans) began to proliferate along the avenues of New York and a wide range of fresh fruits, vegetables, and herbs suddenly were available even in darkest winter. Finally, my husband discovered he wanted to start making bread, which he found entertaining. The bread was and is fantastically good and we eat it without butter, as do all good Francophiles.

Gradually, the new way of eating described in this book began to develop. We both lost weight, felt lighter, and he stopped taking any pills — only a single aspirin twice daily. Our friends seemed sincerely surprised to find us actually looking better. After a few months, when I had accumulated a repertoire of dishes, it became apparent there were other blessings.

One is that low-fat food is superior because it is mostly made up of perfectly fresh foods, from garden, sea, or produce market. These foods are best cooked as soon after harvesting as possible, so I generally do this immediately and serve them up either cold, at room temperature, or reheated. When we have guests, the fetish about all-hot meals is abandoned; instead, we have perhaps a single hot dish, with everything else at room temperature. For example, beginning a winter evening's meal with a bowl of steaming soup establishes a sense of hotness, and once this has been set, the temperature of the remaining dishes is not a vital factor. The cook is free just before dinner.

There is far more diversity of flavor in a low-fat diet than in the old-fashioned, butter-based French cuisine. Herbs and spices are used lavishly, together with astonishing amounts of shallots, garlic, and onions. Condiments from the Near and Far East — sesame seeds, gingerroot, shoyu soy sauce (formerly Tamari, and still known as such in the pages of this book), and Szechuan pepper — liven the palate.

A second boon appeared when I found that low-fat food is very easy to cook. It's virtually never necessary to stand over a hot stove stirring sauces. Nor need the cook hover anxiously over a steak, hoping it won't be ruined by overcooking. Instead, the food processor makes sauces and steaks are a thing of the past.

The food is all basically quick-cooking, in that chicken and fish bake, poach, or broil in anywhere from three to fifteen minutes. Vegetables steam in less time than they take to boil. Whole grains and beans are ready in as much as half an hour or as little as five minutes.

A third bonanza is economic: low-fat is cheaper. Eschewing expensive red meat and cheeses, butter and cream, pastries and virtually all processed foods makes a big difference. The cost of whole grains and beans is minimal, and chicken is far cheaper than meat. We also find it convenient as well as money-saving to make some basic foods at home — bread crumbs, brown sugar, yogurt, and mayonnaise come to mind. Skim-milk yogurt, still somewhat hard to find in the market, is very easy and cheap to make at home.

Before proceeding to the further delights of low-fat living, I want to try to clear up a quite prevalent confusion. A low-salt diet is not at all the same thing as a low-fat one, nor are the reasons for it the same. A low-salt diet is often prescribed for people who have hypertension (high blood pressure). A low-fat diet, on the other hand, is a good preventive as well as a practical treatment for atherosclerosis (clogged arteries). There are dozens of salt-free cookbooks on the market, but the most painless of these must certainly be Craig Claiborne's *Gourmet Diet* (1980).

If your blood pressure is high, your doctor will probably have warned you to avoid salt. This is fairly easy to do if you use other seasonings — the palate adapts quickly — but it's vitally important to stay away from processed foods. These foods, bought in stores, precooked, canned or frozen, are loaded with salt, used as a preservative. Fresh foods, containing only natural salts, are your best bet, and it's with these foods that this low-fat cookbook is primarily concerned. However, if you are on a low-salt diet, be forewarned of two possible problem areas in using this book.

The first is that beans and whole grains, including cereal and bread, are eaten constantly on a low-fat diet and these foods beg to be salted. You may not agree; everyone's tolerance and taste differs. So in most of the recipes where salt is indicated, I've offered an option: "salt, to taste" or "salt, as desired." The second warning has to do with several highly salted seasonings that seem to me to make a low-fat diet work aesthetically. These include anchovies, olives, Parmesan and other low-fat cheeses and, most important, shoyu soy sauce. This sauce, imported from Japan and available here in health-food stores, is made of pure ingredients — soy beans, cracked wheat, and salted water — that have been aged in wood. It is greatly to be preferred to American soy sauces, which are doctored with chemicals. Other salted foods, unsuitable for persons with low-salt needs, appear here often: cottage cheese, tomato juice, canned tuna, and dry skim milk (used to thicken yogurt).

But, happily, salt is unnecessary for seasoning the other vital staple foods in this book: chicken, fish, and vegetables. These foods can be effectively flavored with lemon juice, vinegar, garlic, and a variety of herbs and spices, especially pepper.

One other common cause of confusion has to do with cholesterol. This fatty substance, in amounts necessary for survival, is manufactured in the bodies of humans and animals. Obviously, there is no cholesterol in fruits, grains, or vegetables. I am always surprised by the label "contains no cholesterol" on bottles of vegetable oil, since this would seem self-evident, but what do I know of the vagaries of food manufacturers?

Generally speaking, cholesterol is found in large amounts in foods also high in fats: red meats, cheeses, milk, butter, and cream. If we avoid these foods for the second reason, we have automatically taken care of the first. There are, of course, exceptions. Egg yolks are very high in cholesterol, although relatively low in fat (but that fat happens to be saturated — animal — fat, of which more later).

While it's not entirely proven, as yet, that eating quantities of high-cholesterol foods contributes to high levels of cholesterol in the blood, it seems prudent to avoid them as a general rule. So chicken livers, fish roe, and shrimp are all out-of-bounds. (It's not very difficult to give up shrimp when you consider that most of it arrives at the store frozen and is therefore relatively tasteless, and all of it is fearfully expensive.)

As an exception to the above rule, I include herein a recipe for taramasalata, a delicious dip for hors d'oeuvres made with carp roe. Most recipes recommend 8 ounces of roe, but I find that only a single tablespoon is enough to strongly establish the flavor. The recipe is designed for ten to twelve people, so the amount in any given serving is tiny indeed. The same goes for a single egg yolk, appearing here in three recipes, each planned for from four to ten persons.

With all this talk of avoiding — rather than embracing — foods, I feel as though I've been drawn into a trap. I think of my diet as a pleasure, not a punishment. Quickly, then, I'd like to mention some of the other aberrant foods that we enjoy even though they aren't free of either fat or cholesterol. I've already referred to anchovies, olives, and Parmesan in talking about salt. Other foods that appear here, always for emphasis, and used in moderate amounts, are nuts, seeds, ricotta cheese, and (once) feta cheese.

The diet of an absolute purist is a nightmare, and those who apply themselves to such run the risk of despair and of going off the diet altogether. It's hard enough to give up the red-blooded manly fare we've all been used to, without being asked to give up everything. So, as in the rest of life, the capacity for being flexible is important. If you give yourself sufficient treats and enjoy an occasional fling, you'll be likely to stay within the low-fat precincts for the rest of your life, and find you enjoy them more and more as the years go by.

Which brings me to the question of sugar. We all know it rots the teeth and makes us fat. As long as we aren't asked to give it up altogether, however, it's pretty easy to cut back on it. Because traditional dessert — pies, cakes, pastries, and all chocolate dishes — are full of fat, they are off-limits. But comfort is at hand: there are lots of sweet desserts that have no fat — meringues, macaroons, sherbets, soufflés. You'll find some of these here — an exception being sherbet, hard to make at home and delicious in shops. There are also exciting ways of presenting fruits with sugar in the form of marmalades, honey, or liqueurs, used as liaison and flavoring.

The reduction of fat in the diet makes for basic change. Not only does it affect one's health and appearance, but it seems to influence the substance and style of one's life. For one thing, low-fat food is so easy to prepare that it encourages you to invite guests for meals or drinks, knowing there won't have to be a great outlay of either energy or cash. Entertaining tends to be spontaneous and informal; life becomes more relaxed. It's entirely possible that the innate properties of this food — more natural than man-made — promote not only physical health but spiritual well-being, too.

Much of the ease of preparation must be credited to the food processor. This remarkable invention, available only since the mid-seventies, has revolutionized cooking. It's possible to have grated, thin sliced, or puréed vegetables in seconds. Marinades for chicken and fish, made of a variety of ingredients such as anchovies, mushrooms, and fresh herbs, are completed in a minute. Wonderfully textured fruit desserts — banana freeze and prune soufflé — can be tossed together in practically no time.

One of the greatest advantages of this new way of cooking and eating has already been mentioned: the food needn't be prepared at the last minute, just before meals. The end of the day probably finds you eager for refreshment: you might want to go out for a run or a walk. Perhaps the hour just before dinner is when you want to sit down with a drink and the last thing you want to do is cook.

But cooking can be marvelous — at the time you find right. I love to work concentratedly in the kitchen for an hour or two during the morning or afternoon. It's especially nice to do this when you arrive home with a basketful of fresh food. I like to wash lettuces, dry them carefully (in a plastic spinner), and store them in plastic bags in the refrigerator so they are instantly available for salad. If perfect fresh vegetables have been found in the market, I steam them right away. They can then be served cold, or at room temperature, that day or the next. But their freshness will have been caught, since they were cooked at its height.

If you have a job or a handful at home, you might want to use an odd evening or a stretch of time during the weekend to make a number of different dishes in one session. You then have food on hand that can be used by itself, or in combination with other foods, extending way beyond your immediate needs.

Using a timer to prevent confusion, you can fit yourself into a number of projects. I enjoy working between the stove, the food processor, and the blender. I often poach a chicken, both for the meat (to be used in a variety of dishes) and for the stock, which is a fine base for soup and an all-purpose liquid seasoning. Stock, once it has been defatted, can of course be frozen and quickly thawed when you need it. Invariably, I make a batch of yogurt, and often prepare a dish of beans, if I have been thoughtful earlier on and placed them in a bowl of cold water to soak. Using the food processor, I might chop a jarful of fresh parsley, so it's readily available in the refrigerator. If I have some fresh mushrooms, I might make duxelles from the stalks. (Duxelles, a dry blend of mushrooms and shallots, is a good addition to marinades, stuffing, soups, and sauces.) I generally make soup, which provides us with a main course for lunch or dinner several times a week. I often have melba toast baking slowly in the oven. Occasionally I produce some candied orange peels, made from the rinds of a few oranges — a piquant addition to yogurt and a number of desserts.

All this activity makes for a continuum of foods: the cook needn't ever start from scratch. Low-fat food also means that not only is the refrigerator well stocked, but the kitchen shelves are as well. It's easy to keep whole grains, dried peas and beans, rice, and a variety of pastas on hand at all times. With these basic foods go a variety of condiments, spices, dried herbs, capers, jams. Dried herbs tend to smell like hay after six months, by which time they should be thrown out. But the other foods are all great survivors.

Besides these, we always have ample supplies of shallots, garlic, yellow and red onions, scallions, parsley, carrots, celery, potatoes, lemons, and limes.

The full larder is ultimately economical, but more than that it's a great convenience, as well as a comforting presence in the house. No given meal is an emergency. Instead, there is always a range of simple dishes that can be prepared from indigenous materials. Discreet use of leftovers is a daily affair.

Because most of the work has been done ahead, dinnertime doesn't come as a shock. The cook can feel relaxed, heat up perhaps a single dish, and be confident that the food is going to taste quite wonderful.

The Seasoning Roots

When we first changed from high-fat to low-fat food, the most drastic deprivation was that of butter. It took me a while to realize that although butter is partly used for its liaison properties (as thickening agent, or as binder in making sauces), it's mostly wanted for its taste. Butter appears in the soups, entrées, vegetable courses, and desserts of so-called normal diets. It's always on the table ready to be slathered on bread. To find alternatives for this delicious and ubiquitous substance became a prime project. I began by doubling or tripling the amount of shallots, garlic, or onions indicated in any cookbook recipe. This seemed to be a successful strategy for diverting the attention away from the butter fix.

Shallots are vital. Small, purplish bulbs, they are more delicate than either onions or garlic and need almost no cooking. I buy shallots, for convenience and economy, in one-pound bags at a vegetable market, rather than in those little boxes holding two or three.

In the old days, I bought garlic bulbs one at a time; now I get four. Garlic is a sharp, exciting taste and I like its ability to enhance every dish in which it appears. Like shallots, it cooks in seconds.

We also use a variety of onions. Yellow onions are useful for stuffing poultry and to season robust dishes such as soup and beans. Scallions — green spring onions — are used in their entirety: green leaves and white bulbs. They are particularly valuable in Asian dishes, combined with fresh gingerroot and garlic. Red onions, thinly sliced in the food processor, are excellent in salads, sandwiches, and with beans. White onions are used here only once: poached in white wine and chicken stock, served in their own right.

The Herb Garden and the Spice Rack

Herbs—fresh and dried—are of the essence. Most herbs can be successfully dried, but exceptions have to be made for parsley, basil, and mint. These need to be used fresh or not at all. But other herbs dry very effectively, and come to vivid life when immersed in liquid: marjoram, thyme, dill, oregano, and tarragon.

In winter, in New York and other cities, Asian and other markets stock a number of fresh herbs, including three kinds of parsley: American (curly), Italian (flat-leaved), and Chinese. Chinese parsley is also known as cilantro and sometimes coriander. It looks like Italian parsley, but has a somewhat sharp smell and an acrid taste, which takes a bit of getting used to before you can get to love it. Another way of differentiating Chinese from Italian parsley is that it's sold with its roots intact. Fresh dill is available all winter, too. Although basil and mint can be found, they are apt to be inappropriately expensive. I find I can wait to eat them in summer, when they grow like weeds in our home gardens.

It's so easy to grow your own herbs. All you need is a small patch of earth, or a window box or planter that gets plenty of sun. Basil and parsley can be grown easily from seed, and I find that a single package of seeds is enough for a continuing crop. Once established, basil can be harvested all summer to eat with tomatoes and slices of cold chicken or turkey, to add to salads and fish, and to make pesto for pasta. Parsley, whole or chopped, is tasty, handsome, and full of vitamins, so add it to everything (except desserts) with reckless abandon.

With a little more garden space and less sun, you can have a perennial herb garden, a pleasure in every sense. Thyme, tarragon, oregano, chives, mint, sorrel, and sage return loyally to my sandy piece of ground each spring. Keep cutting these plants so their flowers don't develop and you'll have a perpetual source of fresh herbs to snip just before dinner, to toss into the salad bowl or sprinkle over the fish.

Some of these herbs may be frozen for use over the winter, but they turn limp, even when they retain their flavor. I prefer to confine my freezing to pesto, making numerous jars to carry us through the winter.

It's very easy to dry your own herbs. Cut them first thing in the morning and tie the stems of each variety with string. Hang them upside down in a dry corner of the kitchen. In a couple of weeks they should be ready to be lightly crushed and stored in jars.

Drying herbs can pay off in more ways than one might suspect. One summer when we were trying to sell an old farmhouse in Connecticut there seemed to be no takers. However, one day a woman came in who was so overcome by the charm of the herbs drying in bunches in the kitchen that she sat down forthwith and wrote us out a check.

When using fresh herbs, be extravagant, for they are only half as strong as dried herbs, and since they look as good as they taste, it's nice to use them freely.

Spices are as important as herbs, and they can be cleverly bonded with them. Get used to sniffing and tasting them so that you can make some successful experiments in using them with different foods and combining them with other seasonings.

Of all the spices, pepper is the most important. Always buy it whole and keep it in a pepper grinder so you can have fresh-ground pepper at all times. Tellicherry black pepper is the most pungent. I also keep a pepper grinder full of Szechuan pepper, which I find I use more and more. Heating this pepper in a saucepan, with or without a tiny bit of oil, releases a heavenly smell; the pepper itself has a subtle flavor. White pepper, identical to black except in appearance, is useful for cosmetic purposes: no little black specks mar a white surface.

Unripened peppercorns are green, and they have a delicate flavor, especially suitable with fish. Sold either in freeze-dried form or in a solution, these peppercorns are used only occasionally, but they keep well and are a pleasing variant. Crush them before using them.

Finally, there is red pepper, which is hot and comes in two forms, powdered (cayenne) or crushed. The former is stronger than the latter, but use both sparingly.

Besides pepper, I crush a few other whole spices: cumin, fennel, coriander, and allspice (a single berry that combines the flavors of nutmeg, cinnamon, and clove). For nutmeg, I use a small tin grater, which holds a single nutmeg in a lidded top compartment, and keep it close at hand for quick and frequent seasoning of desserts and some vegetables.

Most of the spices that are good in desserts seem to begin with the letter *c:* cloves, cinnamon, coriander, and cardamom. Cardamom is also a valuable addition to demitasse. Other seasonings you'll find useful in a low-fat kitchen are powdered ginger, English dry mustard (hot), Madras curry powder (combining cumin, coriander, fenugreek, red peppers, and turmeric), Garam Masala (another Indian combination of spices: cardamom, black pepper, cumin, coriander, cinnamon, cloves), and Chinese Five Spices (star anise, fennel, cinnamon bark, cloves, Szechuan pepper).

I find saffron too costly and turmeric too tasteless to justify their inclusion here, although both turn food yellow, which is occasionally desirable. Dijon mustard, which is blended with white wine, makes a lovely, mild seasoning, and it's used constantly throughout this book.

In addition to these natural spices made from seeds and berries, I need to mention again that wonderful Japanese sauce, shoyu (Tamari). And Lea and Perrins Worcestershire sauce and Tabasco (hot pepper) sauce are both useful for jazzing up tomato juice, among other things.

The Acid Fruits

The chefs of the nouvelle cuisine — brilliant innovators — generated a lot of excitement a few years ago about esoteric vinegars, mustards, and honeys. It became fashionable to use vinegars made from raspberries and other unlikely sources. After some rather limited venturing in these fields, I concluded that nothing could be finer than a mild red vinegar, processed in France by Dessaux or Maille. However, since then, I've discovered sherry wine vinegar, from Spain, and find it superior in salad dressing to any other. For white vinegar, I choose a Japanese rice wine vinegar, which is also very mild. Because I prefer my own seasonings, I never buy vinegars flavored with garlic or herbs.

Dry white wine is, itself, a marvelous adjunct to this low-fat cooking: it's part and parcel of many of my chicken and fish dishes. Dry red wine appears in two fruit desserts. And Madeira (or sherry) lends marvelous flavor to black bean soup and — of all things — spinach.

Lemons and limes are used constantly in this cookbook, for both their innate flavor and their ability to draw forth the flavors of other foods.* Lemon juice is often used instead of vinegar in salad dressing, but sometimes in tandem with it.

*To get twice as much juice from a lemon or lime, drop it into boiling water, let it blanch for 1 or 2 minutes, cool it off, and squeeze it. You'll be astonished by the superflux.

Lemon juice is superior for making mayonnaise. Like parsley, lemon peel is an excellent addition to almost any dish.

As to the difference between lemons and limes, it's subtle, but it's there. Lemons are best with fish and chicken, while limes are preferred for desserts and drinks. But for some mysterious reason, the price of lemons rockets up in summer, while limes become abundant and cheap. I go with the music and use them interchangeably.

Striking Oil

Before moving on to the interesting subject of which oils taste best, the large subject of fats — saturated, monounsaturated and polyunsaturated — had better be got out of the way. It's one of the most important parts of this book, and I'll try to pass along what I have learned as simply and clearly as I can.

Saturated fats (bad) tend to be hard at room temperature and are known to raise the levels of cholesterol in the blood. They are found in meat, cheese, butter, egg yolks, chocolate, poultry (think of those big chunks of white fat near a chicken's tail), palm oil, and coconut oil.

Since palm and coconut oil are not used by home cooks, technically we can ignore them. But processed foods are loaded with them, and if you examine the labels of any manufactured foods you are likely to find these oils listed among the ingredients, if sometimes rather ambiguously: "cottonseed *or* palm oils," or "soybean *or* coconut oils" (italics mine). This obviously gives the food processor every sort of advantage, but it also should help persuade you to choose fresh food over any other, every time you go shopping.

Unsaturated fats are a different matter. They tend to be soft at room temperature and it is currently believed that a minimum of one tablespoon a day of polyunsaturated oil actually lowers the level of cholesterol in the blood.

Polyunsaturated fats are present in all the vegetable oils except for two, which are monounsaturated: olive oil and peanut oil. But safflower, corn, sunflower, walnut, and sesame oils are all polyunsaturated, and — used with discretion — are recommended for a low-fat diet.

I find these oils good for cooking because of the variety of flavors available and their already-liquefied state. So I almost never use margarine as a substitute for butter. But if you choose to use it, get tub — rather than stick — margarine. The latter has been hydrogenated, meaning it's been made hard, whereas tub margarine is infused with both air and water to lighten it. The best of the tub margarines is Promise, and a tasty runner-up is Chiffon unsalted.

I always have a half-pound box of whipped sweet butter on hand for any of our friends who want to butter their bread. I seldom have to replace this box oftener than once a month, and find the butter remains fresh.

Monounsaturated fats, found in olive and peanut oil, are currently believed to have no effect, one way or the other, on cholesterol levels in the blood. So, theoretically, one would think we could use them habitually. However, since in a low-fat diet only very limited amounts of *any* fats are used, and since positive effects are associated with small amounts of polyunsaturated fats, it makes sense to use them predominantly. Throughout this book, they are always used in cooked dishes. When, as in salad dressings, the oil is uncooked, I often use part or all olive oil.

In dealing with the two monounsaturated fats, I find I can easily pass up peanut oil, but when it comes to olive oil, I feel compromise is in order. The strong, Mediterranean flavor of olive oil is a positive addition to many uncooked foods, such as salad dressing and pesto. Happily, its taste dominates even when olive oil is combined with other, blander oils. (See Less is More, page 28.)

For mayonnaise, and also for general cooking, safflower oil is perfectly satisfactory and its ratio of polyunsaturated to saturated fats is superior to that of any other oil (it's actually 11 to 1). The other polyunsaturated oils I use often are corn oil and walnut oil, the latter a particularly felicitous addition to salads and cold string beans. Strong, and delicious-tasting, sesame oil is so powerful that only a few drops can have an astonishing effect, and like olive oil, it enhances other oils when used in combination with them.

Although vegetable fats are used principally in this book, we also depend on a few dairy products. We eat them by themselves or use them in combination with other foods.

Skim-milk yogurt is a cornerstone of a low-fat diet. When buying yogurt or any other dairy products, keep a sharp eye on labels. They can be deceptive. For instance, "regular" yogurt contains 7 percent butterfat. Skim-milk yogurt has less than 1 percent. In between these two, you will find "low-fat" yogurt that contains as much as 4 percent butterfat, admittedly less than the "regular" version has, but a lot more than in the skim-milk kind.

Cottage cheese can contain as little as one half of 1 percent butterfat, but it's very dry: I couldn't recommend it. Cottage cheese with either 1 percent or 2 percent butterfat is splendid. It makes a good dish for lunch, accompanied by some toast, a sliced tomato, and a sprig of watercress.

Also, cottage cheese can be blended with yogurt in the food processor, and the resulting mixture makes a good dip for raw vegetables as a substitute for sour cream. See page 53 for recipe.

Parmesan cheese is the only hard cheese we eat, the reason being that it's partly made of skim milk and also that a very little of it goes a long way. When freshly grated (in the food processor or blender), Parmesan expands hugely.

Buttermilk is a marvelous drink, which contains very little fat but tastes rich and luxurious. We find it goes very well at lunchtime, especially in summer, when we take it to the beach with cucumber sandwiches. It's also good in soup (see Buttermilk Soup, page 68, and Sweet Potato Soup, page 76) and excellent for making pancakes. Get the kind that specifies a low fat content; i.e., 1½ percent.

Mozzarella is a soft, low-fat Italian cooking cheese, and it's used here occasionally in small quantities. It's good in cornmeal and in a low-fat version of eggplant parmigiana (page 133). It also goes well with fresh basil and chopped tomatoes in a summertime salad. Some Italian stores get daily deliveries of fresh mozzarella (both plain and smoked), and this is an occasional treat worth having. But ordinarily commercial mozzarella from the supermarket does fine and, fortunately, it comes in two versions: one made partly with skim milk, and the other made entirely of whole milk. Obviously, we opt for the skim-milk version and it's nice to find there is virtually no difference in either taste or texture.

I save until last my favorite. Ricotta cheese is so light, sweet, and delectable that I feel it's like eating clouds. Even though it is highest in butterfat of any of the cheeses in this section, it's comforting to recognize that it's still got only one-third the amount found in something as ordinary (and rubbery) as plain old cream cheese. Like mozzarella, ricotta is made commercially in a skim-milk version. When you buy it, be sure the expiration date on the bottom is at least a month away. Also like mozzarella, ricotta can be found freshly made in Italian shops, and should you be having a dinner party and want an effortless and very special dessert, get a pound. If you top off a scoop of ricotta with Kahlua (the Mexican coffee liqueur) and a sprinkling of candied orange peel, you will have an instant dessert to sustain your soul and convince your friends of the lush possibilities of a low-fat diet.

To Market to Market

Although the preparation of food in this book is simplicity itself (compared to other cookbooks), the shopping is somewhat more demanding. When you don't use butter for a primary flavor, you have to seek out a variety of vital and exciting seasonings. This means shopping around, always being on the lookout for the freshest and tastiest ingredients.

The best fruits and vegetables are now found at green markets, where farmers bring their produce directly to the public, and in small shops, often operated by Koreans who have recently arrived in this country. In New York, these shops have multiplied over the past few years to the point where they have affected our supermarkets. The latter are now paying more attention to their produce departments, sometimes even using barrels and baskets for display purposes to underscore the natural look of fresh food. This is a far cry from the plastic-wrapped packages of stale vegetables of a few years ago.

Supermarkets now also stock a variety of foods that used to be somewhat hard to find. Usually they have a wide variety of dried peas and beans, pita bread, brown rice, Dijon mustard, and imported teas. In these stores, we get all our dairy foods, chicken, and at the delicatessen counter an occasional package of baked ham, freshly sliced, to use judiciously in a couple of grain dishes.

In New York, freshly made bread — French, Italian, and German — can be found all over town. Good pita bread is often sold in supermarkets, as well as in Middle Eastern specialty shops. Superb whole-grain bread, made in Pennsylvania, is also found in many supermarkets. We use the less pure but very useful American breads, which we buy extra-thin-sliced: whole wheat, multigrain, Jewish rye, and white. The latter is invaluable for cucumber sandwiches, melba toast, and as an ingredient in taramasalata (page 45).

The Korean shops, once confined to fresh fruits and vegetables, are now expanding and stocking up with groceries, including pasta and a wide range of exotic seasonings. I get sesame oil, chili oil, and Szechuan pepper there, as well as fresh gingerroot, candied ginger, bags of almonds and quantities of shallots.

Italian shops are the best source for fresh Parmigiano-Reggiano cheese, which it's good to buy a pound at a time and grate as needed, and for crusty Italian bread, which is delivered daily. Here one can also buy imported Italian canned tomatoes, sun-dried tomatoes, and tomato paste sold in convenient tubes that are not always easy to find in supermarkets. Dried Italian pasta is apt to be freshest here, where the demand is greatest: the DeCecco brand is first-rate.

It's helpful to make an occasional visit to one of the international food bazaars (Dean and DeLuca or Zabar's in New York) and stock up. I like Dundee marmalade, packed in stone jars in Scotland. Also in these stores are a variety of vinegars, water-processed decaffeinated coffee beans, Chinese teas — of which my favorite is a Lapsang Souchong called Hu-Kwa, packaged in Boston. In the refrigerator, you can usually find jars of tarama, which is carp-roe paste; using the recipe for taramasalata here (page 45), you'll find that one jar will probably last you six months.

Fish is a tricky business, requiring much research. It's expensive, and if it has either been frozen or been lying around the store for a few days, it's worthless. Recently, many fish stores have begun solving this problem by adding a restaurant, or hiring a cook, so they can sell prepared dishes made from the unbought fish. If you find a reliable fish market, make yourself known, and give them as much business as you can. Learn about local fish, and on which days it is delivered. Make friends with the salespeople and tell them you depend on them to give you only the very freshest fish.

Health-food stores are valuable for a number of foods hard to find elsewhere. Bulgur (coarsely cracked wheat) is sold both in bulk and in packages. I buy several pounds at a time; it keeps well and is a delicious, timesaving food. Other grains, as well as dried peas and beans, nuts and seeds, are also available in bulk at these shops, at prices comparable to those in supermarkets.

Shoyu Tamari sauce is a staple of health-food stores. Middle Eastern sesame seed paste (tahini) is milder than the Asian variety, and good for making hummous. But stay away from the sesame oil, which is quite tasteless; instead, get yours in an Asian shop. Walnut oil, on the other hand, is fine here. It's a good idea to avoid the organically grown vegetables. In general they're so costly that no one wants them, and they tend to be elderly and exhausted after their long wait for buyers. But if you are a bread maker, this is the place to get fresh yeast.

Cool It

Almost everything keeps best in a cool place, and often this is the refrigerator or freezer. If we all stored food as we should, we'd have to double the size of the equipment currently in our kitchens. Since we aren't likely to do this right away, we need to choose what foods deserve the best treatment.

Parmesan cheese, well wrapped in several layers of plastic or aluminum foil, keeps fresh on the bottom shelf — the coldest part — of the refrigerator. Grate a chunk in the food processor just before using it. If you have any grated cheese left over, freeze it.

Coffee keeps best in the freezer, and so do nuts, but here things begin to get crowded — for already you have chicken, bread, orange juice, and leftovers stored there. Save a little space for sliced bananas in a plastic container so you can always make banana freeze (page 190).

In the refrigerator, Chinese parsley will keep fresh if you put the whole bunch into a tall glass, half filled with water. Place a plastic bag loosely over the leaves.

Mushrooms should be eaten within a day or two of being bought. Keep them lightly covered, so the air can get to them.

Well-washed lettuces and fresh herbs keep wonderfully in plastic bags if you introduce air into each bag before sealing. Hold the bag by its two top corners and swing it around in the air until it swells out. Then, quickly, tie the ends together.

Of the root vegetables, onions and garlic do fine out in the open, but shallots and scallions need the dark and cold of the vegetable bin.

Whole wheat flour, used in bread and for pancake mix, needs to be kept in the refrigerator in hot weather. Obviously, the pancake mix also needs to be kept cold, as do opened bottles of maple syrup.

Enough!

No Place Like Home

It's an enormous satisfaction to be able to make certain foods at home and mayonnaise is a perfect example. It is accomplished in a couple of minutes using the food processor (see page 26). Its taste is superior to that of any store-bought mayonnaise, it's free of preservatives, always available, and, of course, cheaper.

Yogurt, made with skim milk, never fails when it's made in a quart jar, and enclosed in a vacuum container for an overnight rest. I never had any luck trying to keep yogurt protected in an unlit oven, or any pleasure in using those five fussy little jars, but with a Solait (see page 27) making yogurt at home is a dream (page 52). The three small steps involved take place over a period of forty minutes, so I often make a batch of yogurt when I am in the kitchen anyway, cooking other things at the same time, and scarcely notice I'm doing it.

Bread crumbs are instantly produced when one or two slices of fresh bread, torn into pieces, are minced in the food processor or blender.

Brown sugar is created by stirring a tablespoon of molasses into ½ cup of white sugar, and mixing thoroughly. (This keeps perfectly in the refrigerator.)

Melba toast is wonderfully easy to make, and can be stored for weeks in a glass jar or tin canister. See the nearly effortless directions for this on page 40.

Seltzer water can be made at home using a siphon. You can buy one of these at a department or hardware store, together with a box of cartridges. This is a convenience — much easier than shopping for, and lugging home, a lot of heavy bottles. In states with bottle laws, this can mean lugging the empties back. Again, there is an ultimate economy: seltzer made at home costs half as much as that in the shops.

Tools of the Trade

If you are serious about going on a low-fat diet, you're going to immediately gain a lot of new space in your kitchen. Out go all those frying pans (keeping only one small iron one for candied orange peels), together with the cake tins, pie plates, cookie cutters, and rolling pins.

But there is one important piece of equipment you are going to need and that is a food processor. I wouldn't dare suggest that anyone try to cope with this new method of cooking without it. A food processor of excellent quality can be bought these days for $100 or less. If this seems to you an extravagance, remember that the machine will begin paying for itself the day you decide to go on a low-fat diet.

In seconds, a food processor grates raw carrots and zucchini; chops onions, shallots, herbs, and mushrooms; slices cucumbers and apples; blends sauces and marinades; and makes puréed vegetables a part of everyday life. In other words, it provides us with a far more adventurous and varied diet than we could have dreamed of in the old days before its invention.

As to directions and hints for using a food processor, study the manual that comes with a new machine, and you'll find yourself at home with it within two weeks' time. Working with carrots, incidentally, is a good way to learn about this machine's great versatility.

A steamer for cooking vegetables is vital. The small steel baskets that fit into other pots strike me as inefficient. I greatly prefer a generous two-tiered steaming pot, where you can steam potatoes in the bottom layer and, later, add a tray of quick-cooking vegetables on the top. These steamers can be found in kitchen supply shops. I got mine, made of metal, in a Chinese supermarket for $15. The advantages of steaming are numerous. Vegetables keep their color and vitamins, they never become soggy with water, they retain their moisture so the need for butter is obviated.

Nonstick pans are a fantastic invention, particularly adapted to low-fat cooking. Coated with a strong sealing agent (Silverstone is the American brand), these pans cook foods without any fat. Consequently, they are very easy to keep clean. Three sizes are essential: one small sautéing pan is used constantly for shallots and onions. A large sautéing pan is needed for pancakes, and chicken curry. A third pan, a 1½-quart saucepan, is necessary for cooking cereal and rice; it's also used to heat the milk for yogurt.

The vacuum container for making yogurt, mentioned earlier, is manufactured by two companies in the USA. Mine is a Solait, made by the Crayon Yard Corporation in New Haven, Connecticut 06519. A similar one can be ordered from Finesse, Ltd., Box 734, Carmel, California 93924. Both cost in the neighborhood of $25 and are worth it.

A sturdy garlic press makes one clove do the work of two or three. A Swiss-made Susi press is in constant use in my kitchen. Get it or any well-made garlic press in a kitchen supply store.

A wire rack is needed for roasting poultry. The rack, available at most ten-cent stores, elevates the bird above all that fat dripping into the pan.

A plastic salad spinner, costing about $8, is a must. Drying lettuce with paper towels is archaic.

A small wooden mortar and pestle, good for crushing whole spices, is available in Chinese stores. Expensive small spice grinders can be bought if you insist.

The blender is such a familiar tool that I mention it last. It's perfect for making soup. Otherwise, it's no substitute for the food processor and vice versa. You definitely need both.

As convenient on a low-fat diet as on any other are enamel-lined iron pots, imported or domestic, which are useful for both cooking and serving. It's nice to have them in several sizes, but a 3-quart one is indicated here for dishes designed for eight people.

Less Is More

It may be a dubious analogy, but I think that this architectural principle of Mies van der Rohe can usefully be applied to food. For example, the essence of orange juice (or a building) is best revealed by emphasizing the basic material. So even though frozen orange juice may be as nutritious as fresh (drunk immediately after opening), the flavor is inferior. But add the juice of one fresh, whole orange to a pitcher of frozen juice, and the natural flavor is amazing — it immediately dominates the whole.

In the same way, a teaspoon or tablespoon of half-and-half, added to the skim milk on the morning cereal, makes the whole dish taste creamy.

When olive oil is joined with one of the bland vegetable oils, it asserts its superiority and its flavor becomes the controlling one.

A final example deals with quantity rather than quality, but it still works. Salad dressing is most effective when a small amount of it is used. When lettuce leaves merely gleam with a light coat of dressing, the salad itself assumes its proper importance.

Sense and Sensibility

As the nutritional advantages of this diet are so tremendous (and felt to be, in this house, actually lifesaving), it might seem ungrateful to stress from now on the other aspects of the food: its looks, smells, tastes, and textures. But we all eat and enjoy *food,* not chemical components, and so it's the aesthetic values — once we've accepted the basic premises — that come to be the dominant ones.

For this reason, you won't find any lists of calories, or cholesterol or fat content, appended to the recipes in this book. I've always been put off by their inclusion in diet books, feeling them to be redundant, as well as distasteful. By this time, it would seem that both you and I have done the hard work:

learned the new restrictions, made the decision to change the way we eat, and begun to shop in a somewhat unaccustomed manner.

So now it would seem appropriate to relax, rejoice, and cook some marvelous dishes.

Breakfast

Breakfast can be a delicious meal, taking only minutes to cook, but it will sustain you until lunchtime, at which point you will be normally hungry rather than ravenous.

In winter, hot cereal is the heart of the matter. It's comforting food that soon becomes indispensable. We usually have either oatmeal or Wheatena. It's important to buy "regular" cereal, never the "instant" variety, as the latter is full of salt and inferior in flavor. Combine cereal in a nonstick saucepan with water and a little salt, if you need it. Bring it to a boil, give it a stir, reduce heat to a simmer, and in a few minutes it will be thick and ready to eat. We have it with skim milk, to which I add a tablespoon (or less) of half-and-half — this makes the skim milk taste rich and creamy.

Grapefruit is the other wintertime breakfast essential. While the cereal is cooking, slice one in half, and heat up the water for coffee or tea. Occasionally, it's nice to have toasted bagels or English muffins, perhaps with jam, and some juice — either orange, grapefruit, or tomato.

In summer, we switch to cold cereal: Nutri-Grain, Shredded Wheat, and Grape Nuts are all delicious and free of sugar. I like to add raisins or a sliced banana. We replace the grapefruit with melon, or sliced peaches. We sometimes have toast (raisin toast is big, here) and iced coffee or tea.

On Sunday mornings, in the American way (and particularly when we have houseguests), we have pancakes.

PANCAKE MIX

Lest the production of pancakes appear difficult, let me hurriedly say that I make a big batch of pancake mix ahead of time — in one of those marathon kitchen sessions:

2 cups unbleached flour	3 teaspoons baking soda
1 tablespoon salt	1 tablespoon sugar
2 teaspoons baking powder	4 cups whole wheat flour

Sift the unbleached flour into a big bowl — using a sifter, if you have one, or a strainer, if you don't. Then spoon it back into a big measuring cup, add the salt, baking powder, sugar, and soda, and resift it. Then gently add the whole wheat flour and stir the mixture thoroughly. Store in a plastic container in the refrigerator until you're ready to use it.

PANCAKES
(Serves 4)

1 cup pancake mix
1½ cups buttermilk
2 egg whites

Mix these together lightly — don't blend them. Drop the batter into a preheated nonstick pan, and grill the pancakes for about 3 minutes on each side. Serve them with pure maple syrup or molasses. When blueberries are in season, ¼ cup of tiny ones added to a batch of pancakes often brings little cries of pleasure from the assembled group.

GRANOLA

Good year-round, Granola is nice to mix with dry cereals such as Nutri-Grain or to sprinkle on yogurt. Make it at home, for the stuff sold in health-food stores is full of sugary additives. It takes 2 minutes to mix and 15 minutes to cook.

2–3 cups rolled oats	2 tablespoons honey
1 cup wheat germ	2 tablespoons oil
½ cup raw sunflower seeds	2 tablespoons raisins
¼ cup sesame seeds	

Put all ingredients except raisins in a large bowl. After mixing well, bake in roasting pan in 300° oven for 15 minutes. Every 5 minutes, open oven to stir granola thoroughly, so all parts of it get brown and crisp. Cool, and then add a scattering of raisins. Store in a big glass jar. This will last for weeks.

FRUIT AND VEGETABLE JUICES

Frozen juices contain as many vitamins as fresh, provided they are drunk as soon as the can is opened. Mixed with fresh juice (as in the morning orange juice), the taste is improved mightily. A single fresh orange can dominate a can of frozen juice.

Tomato juice is a wonderful drink, sold in cans or (better) in bottles. Avoid the kind that admits it is "made from concentrate." Tomato juice is improved by blending into it two or three fresh or canned tomatoes, some Lea and Perrins Worcestershire sauce, Tabasco, and a little cumin, freshly ground. Some oregano, fresh or dried, makes a nice final touch.

COFFEE

We drink mostly decaffeinated these days, and the best of this has been processed with water and then is freshly ground. However, Medaglia d'Oro makes a highly successful decaffeinated brew that is especially good after dinner, with a pinch of cardamom and a sliver of lemon peel.

We also mix coffees, regular with decaffeinated and Italian with American. It's nice to occasionally serve coffee with hot skim milk, or with skim milk beaten to a froth in the blender.

By adding a little cinnamon to this brew, you make, of course, cappuccino.

TEA

Chinese teas, imported by the British, can now be found in supermarkets, along with herb teas that are much favored by young people.

Myself, I have a longtime affection for Lapsang souchong, and particularly fancy one packaged in Boston called Hu-Kwa. In summer, it makes superior iced tea.

ICED TEA
(Serves 4)

5 teaspoons Lapsang souchong tea
4 cups boiling water
1 6-ounce can frozen lemonade

Put the lemonade in the bottom of a pitcher, and strain the hot tea (brewed for 5 minutes) over it. Serve in ice-filled glasses with a sprig of mint.

Drinks and
Hors d'Oeuvres

At the twilight hour, there are many pleasant things to do, one of which is to invite ten or twelve friends in for a glass and something good to eat. It's an easy way to entertain; you can afford odd mixes of people, without endangering an entire evening. People feel free to talk and mingle when they know there is a definite time limit; they can't be trapped.

The food should be light: seeds, nuts, olives, crisp raw vegetables, perhaps a dip or two with some thin crackers. Other, more elaborate offerings are described on pages 46–48: stuffed mushrooms, marinated mussels, fish mousse. As to drinks, more and more people are asking for white wine, to mix with soda (spritzer) or with cassis (oddly called kir). Campari and vermouths, both dry and sweet, are becoming more popular than Scotch and vodka.

Seltzer, which is pure sparkling water (unlike club soda, which contains additives), is in great demand. Lots of people drink it plain, with a slice of lime. We used to order seltzer by the case, in New York, but now we have a siphon bottle, reminiscent of twenties movies. It uses small cartridges to charge tap water. This is a space as well as a labor saver, since it means you can avoid lugging heavy bottles back and forth to the grocery store. When we have gatherings, we also use regular store bottles of seltzer, so as not to have to interrupt the proceedings to run up a fresh supply.

Diet quinine is preferable to "regular" tonic, since it contains less sugar, sodium, and other additives. (Compare the labels when you buy tonic next time.)

Drinks and Hors d'Oeuvres   39

Although one would think that diluting wine with seltzer would make it less intoxicating, the opposite seems to be true; spritzer is exhilarating in a way that a plain glass of wine is not. There must be a hidden truth here, otherwise why would beer be the most popular drink in the world and champagne the most exciting?

CRACKERS AND TIDBITS

Imported crackers are generally low in fat and occasionally fat-free. We like the crisp and tasty offerings from Scandinavia: Wasa, Ideal, Finn Crisp, and Sprodbrod, as well as others from France (Cracottes) and England (Ryvita). We also have fat-free matzo from the United States, where, otherwise, all crackers are loaded with fats.

Pita bread, the unleavened bread of the Middle East (served there in cafés with dishes of tahini), contains no fat. Try to find a brand made by a small firm of recent immigrants. When they become successful, these groups tend to be absorbed by large American companies and the resulting bread is apt to be thick and heavy. If you can find some very fresh pita bread, tear it apart and then cut the pieces into appropriate sizes. Eat it as is. Most of the time, however, pita bread is improved by light toasting.

Melba toast — made at home out of very thin sliced bread — is delectable. Use white, rye, or whole wheat bread, or all three. Cut squares or triangles out of half a stacked loaf. In a 300° oven, heat them for 20 minutes on cookie sheets in the top part of the oven. Cool and store in a glass jar.

Sunflower seeds are lovely to nibble. Pour 2 cups of them into a roasting pan, sprinkle on ¼ teaspoon of shoyu Tamari sauce, stir them around, and bake in a 300° oven for 10 minutes. Eat them slowly.

A dish of shelled walnuts is a steady favorite. This is nice because walnuts are very low in (of course, unsaturated) fat and also require no preparation whatever.

However, almonds, which are superior, do need treatment.

I like them so much that I roast a pound of almonds every so often and then dole them out rather sparingly at small parties. They need to be skinned: pour boiling water over the almonds and let them sit for a couple of minutes. Drain them, and you'll find their skins slip off easily. Heat the oven to 400°, spread the almonds over a large pan, and roast them for 15 minutes. Turn them with a spatula at 5-minute intervals. Salt them or not, as you wish. They are sumptuous, either way.

Raisins are always pleasing at any time of day or night, and candied ginger is a good after-dinner sweet. Kumquats, in winter, look pretty nestled in a dish with their leaves, and they taste marvelous. A dish of dried apricots is a luxurious offering on the all-purpose coffee table.

The best olives in the world are ripe green ones, but they are dreadfully expensive. Black Greek olives are too oily for eating with one's fingers, so we usually settle for excellent Spanish green olives, stuffed with pimiento, and are grateful for our blessings.

RAW VEGETABLES

Crunchy and colorful, raw vegetables look and taste good People tend to eat compulsively when they're drinking before dinner (I know I do) and you feel much better in the morning after you've gorged on cucumbers rather than Gorgonzola.

Beets, cold, quartered, pierced with a toothpick, are unusual hors d'oeuvres. Boil them in their skins for 1 hour, chill them; the skins slip off easily. Serve them exactly as they are.

Carrots and celery are really too obvious to mention. But slim carrot sticks are splendidly crunchy. And celery stalks, cut into one-inch lengths after being stuffed with a cottage cheese sauce (see page 52) are ever dependable.

Cauliflower and broccoli are excellent raw if they are young and freshly picked. (Otherwise, they may be steamed briefly and then chilled.)

Cherry tomatoes need to be well salted. To honor your salt-wary friends, you might serve tomatoes plain, accompanied by a small dish of coarse salt for dipping.

Cucumbers, cut into long strips, can be served with a dip — herb-seasoned cottage cheese and yogurt, for instance (see page 53). Better are rounds of cucumber slices, on quartered pieces of bread that have been lightly stroked with yogurt mayonnaise (page 55). Top these with a fresh mint leaf.

Belgian endive is abundant and, therefore, cheap in late winter. Buy a lot to use in salads and also to serve for hors d'oeuvres. Gently pull apart the leaves and then stand them up in a tall glass, their tips immersed in a light vinaigrette made of oil, a few drops of vinegar, and pepper.

Fennel is another wintertime vegetable, usually eaten raw. The freshest fennel is identifiable by its long stalks, which have feathery tips. Slice the fennel bulb either vertically or horizontally, but do this just before serving it, so it doesn't discolor.

Green beans, blanched and chilled, are superb when they are young and tender. Older beans are unsuitable for hors d'oeuvres.

Mushrooms, fresh and white, are crisp eaten raw. Their flavor is unlike anything else. Depending on their size, serve them whole or halved.

Peppers come in a variety of colors — green (the most common), red (a ripened and somewhat sweeter pepper), and another ripe version in a beautiful shade of yellow. Slice them into slim strips, getting rid of all the seeds and paring away all the white integument. Arrange them in groups for emphasis.

Red radishes are crisp and tart only when they are absolutely fresh, still attached to unblemished green leaves. Clip their tops and bottoms and arrange a bowl of several bunches for a party, using the leaves as support. Serve these with a bowl of coarse salt.

Scallions, with their roots and a third of their green tops cut off, make an excellent addition to a bowl of chilled vegetables.

Snow peas are still somewhat unusual as hors d'oeuvres and this is a recommendation. They have fine color, crisp texture, and a sweet, delicate flavor. Nip off the tips and serve them whole.

White radishes, a.k.a. daikon, make an exotic appearance. Buy them in Asian markets, and serve them plain or with a little bowl of Tamari sauce.

Zucchini, unpeeled and cut in slender strips, are ideal vegetables to serve with a dip such as Taramasalata or well-seasoned yogurt mayonnaise.

A VARIETY OF DIPS

Four dips follow, three of them Mediterranean favorites. They are good with crackers, melba toast, or pita bread.

HUMMOUS
(Serves 10)

Middle Eastern peanut butter — tahini (sesame seed paste) — is combined with cooked chick-peas to make a delicious dip to serve with fresh pita bread or crackers. It is also good to spread on toast.

2 cups cooked chick-peas (page 84) *plus*	**2 tablespoons lemon juice**
1 cup of their cooking water	**3 garlic cloves, minced**
3 tablespoons tahini	**1 teaspoon fresh-ground cumin**
1 tablespoon olive oil	**¼ teaspoon cayenne pepper**

In food processor, whirl the cooked chick-peas with ½ cup of the water, together with the other ingredients. Add more water if necessary to create a smooth texture. Chill and serve topped with a sprig of parsley.

EGGPLANT PURÉE
(Serves 10)

Everyone likes this dip. It is a fair companion for toasted pita bread or Scandinavian crackers; or you can serve it as a separate dish at a buffet supper.

First, pierce an eggplant with a fork in several places and then steam it for 15 minutes or so. When it is completely limp and soft, allow it to cool. Then peel off the skin in large strips.

1 eggplant (about 1 pound),
  steamed and peeled
2 garlic cloves
2 thin slices gingerroot

1 tablespoon brown sugar*
1 tablespoon red wine vinegar

Peel garlic and gingerroot and mince them well in the food processor. Add eggplant and the other ingredients, and whip these to a soft paste. Chill in the refrigerator for a few hours, if possible, to enhance the flavor.

*See page 25 for directions for making brown sugar at home in one minute.

TAPENADE
(Serves 10)

Like hummous (page 43) and taramasalata (page 45), tapenade is a favorite appetizer in the Mediterranean basin. It is easily made in a food processor. Keep the essential ingredients on hand at all times, and you will never be at a loss for a last-minute dish for a party. If you or your guests have problems about sodium, skip this recipe.

1 6½-ounce can solid or
  chunk white tuna, packed
  in water
1 can anchovies (flat)
2 tablespoons capers
2–3 cloves garlic, peeled
1 small onion, peeled
10 black Greek olives, pitted

1 tablespoon lemon juice
1 tablespoon olive oil
chopped fresh parsley and
  thyme
1 tablespoon brandy (op-
  tional)

Drain and rinse tuna and anchovies. Whirl everything together in the food processor and chill well before serving.

TARAMASALATA
(Serves 10)

This is a pale pink dip that has a delicacy and piquancy quite
unlike anything else. Buy a jar of carp-roe paste in a Greek or
Italian shop, or look in the refrigerator at a gourmet bazaar.
It is cheap, and very little is needed to create an effect. Keep
the jar in your refrigerator for later use.

This dip is convenient because it can be made in 15 minutes if you also remember to keep some thin-sliced white
bread in the freezer at all times.

6 slices thin-sliced white
  bread
¾ cup skim milk
2 or 3 small garlic cloves,
  minced

3 tablespoons lemon juice
2 tablespoons corn or safflower oil
1 tablespoon carp-roe paste

Tear the bread into pieces and soak it in the milk for 10
minutes. Drain and squeeze dry in a clean dish towel, press-
ing all the excess milk out of the bread. Put the bread and the
other ingredients into the food processor and whirl them
until they are perfectly smooth. This might take from 1 to 2
minutes.

POPCORN

Popcorn needs no butter to be absolutely delicious, and you can make it at home with ease. Just ½ cup of kernels makes a big bowlful of popcorn. This is, incidentally, a moderately nutritious snack and one that both children and grown-ups eat up.

In a large pot, heat 1 teaspoon of oil and 2 grains of corn. Cover the pot, and when you hear the first pop, toss in the remainder of the corn. Shake the pan occasionally as you cook it over low heat, until all the grains have popped and the pot is quiet. This shouldn't take more than 4 minutes. Sprinkle the popped corn with some fine-ground salt and watch it disappear.

STUFFED MUSHROOMS
(Serves 10)

These make an elegant appearance, and taste wonderful. Carefully choose perfectly fresh, medium-sized mushrooms. Buy them only if their tops are snow white and curl up around the stems so their brown undersides are invisible. Allow 3 mushrooms per person.

At home, wipe the mushroom tops with a damp rag or sponge, and scoop out the stalks. These can either be incorporated into the stuffing, or put aside to make into duxelles (see page 135).

A cupful of stuffing will be enough to fill 30 mushroom caps. The possibilities here are endless. Explore your refrigerator to see if you have any leftover bits of chicken or cooked fish, or some extra dip (cottage cheese and yogurt, or taramasalata).

Put whatever you have in the food processor, add a clove of garlic or a shallot, and a handful of fresh herbs, if available: parsley, dill, marjoram, or tarragon. Season with fresh-ground pepper, lemon juice, or salt.

Taste what you have, and when the substance suits you, fill

each mushroom cap using a tiny spoon or butter knife. Arrange them on a platter and chill.

COLD MUSSELS
(Serves 8)

These mussels make great hors d'oeuvres. Served cold, speared on toothpicks, each one makes a delicate mouthful. Wash 4 pounds of mussels in several cold-water baths until the water is clear, and all sand and dirt has been removed. Don't bother to cut off the beards or scrape off any clinging barnacles: they will take care of themselves during the steaming process. If you plan to use the broth for soup (it combines happily with chicken stock) or as a medium for cooking rice, strain it before proceeding.

Put ½ cup white wine or vermouth in the bottom of a large pot, add the mussels, cover the pot, and steam the mussels until they open. This will take 5 minutes or so. Cool the mussels and remove the meat from the shells; keep it cold while you prepare the marinade:

1 tablespoon minced shallots	2 tablespoons dry vermouth
	1 tablespoon Dijon mustard
3 tablespoons minced fresh parsley and thyme	pinch of ground fennel seed
	fresh-ground black pepper
1 tablespoon lemon juice	
2 tablespoons corn or safflower oil	

Chop shallots and herbs in the food processor. Add the lemon juice, oil, vermouth, and other seasonings, and blend. Pour over the mussels. Chill for an hour or so. Drain before serving, on a platter, with toothpicks.

SZECHUAN FISH MOUSSE
(Serves 12 to 20)

One of the easiest to prepare of the dishes in this book, this mousse makes a terrific hit at parties — either at the cocktail hour or as one of an array of platters for a buffet supper. Present it cold, neatly mounded, decorated with black Greek olives or a few leaves of fresh oregano. Melba toast is a suitable accompaniment.

2 pounds fresh codfish
3–4 cloves garlic, minced
4 tablespoons oil (partly olive oil)
4 tablespoons low-fat cottage cheese
4 tablespoons skim milk

1 teaspoon crushed Szechuan peppercorns
½ teaspoon Chinese Five Spices°
10 pitted Greek black olives (or fresh oregano leaves), for garnish

Over boiling water, steam a large filet of codfish (or 2 pounds of tongues and cheeks) for 5 minutes. Spread fish out onto a large platter and extract any bits of bone or pieces of skin.

Purée the fish in the food processor with the oil and minced garlic. Add the other ingredients and blend well. Arrange as suggested above, and chill the mousse until you're ready to serve it up.

°Chinese Five Spices is described on page 16.

Yogurt and Other Sauces

Skim-milk yogurt is an essential food in a low-fat diet. It is both a dish in itself and a liaison connecting other foods to each other. At breakfast, yogurt is good topped with home-made granola (page 34). At lunch or supper, yogurt is an important complement to beans or whole grains. By itself it is a cool and refreshing dessert, when topped off with fresh-ground gingerroot, or combined with fresh fruit.

As a liaison, skim-milk yogurt combines with cottage cheese to make sauces reminiscent of both cream cheese and sour cream. Combined with mayonnaise, in equal amounts (and seasoned only with Dijon mustard), yogurt is a superb dip for raw vegetables. Blended with ricotta cheese, yogurt turns into a splendid sauce for desserts.

Americans resisted yogurt for years until the Dannon Company cleverly introduced some jam into each carton. Other companies followed suit, and sweetened yogurt has become nearly as popular as ice cream. If you want to follow this route and — I hope — slowly work your way back to the pure basic product, buy plain skim-milk yogurt and add your own jam.

Also in this section are a number of other sauces: vinaigrette and buttermilk dressings for salads, tomato sauces made of fresh and canned tomatoes, and pesto, the marvelous Italian sauce made of fresh basil, first used with pasta, and now appearing in all kinds of places.

HOMEMADE SKIM-MILK YOGURT

We make yogurt constantly, but scarcely realize we are doing it because it has become so habitual. Whenever we are in the kitchen preparing a meal or cooking a batch of other foods, it's a simple matter to make a quart of yogurt.

The secret of this lies in a single piece of equipment. It is a specially designed thermal cylinder that holds a glass quart jar. This nonelectrical device provides perfect insulation for yogurt's ripening and cooling process. (For source, see page 27.)

1 quart skim milk
4 tablespoons dry skim milk (for thickening)
2 tablespoons yogurt (for starter), at room temperature

Combine the liquid and dry milks in a nonstick saucepan, stir well, and heat them over a moderate flame to just below the boiling point. At sea level this takes 10 minutes: set the timer.

When milk begins to simmer, remove pot from the stove and reset the timer for 30 minutes, by which time the milk will be lukewarm. Put 2 tablespoons starter into a quart-sized measuring cup or saucepan. Pour a small amount of hot milk over the starter and stir well. Add the rest of the milk and gently mix before pouring the yogurt into the glass quart jar. Or pour it through a strainer (mashing down the curds with a wooden spoon) into a quart-sized measuring cup, and pour strained yogurt into the glass jar.

Cap the jar, insert it into the plastic container, and put the whole thing into the refrigerator. The yogurt will be thick and cool about 15 hours later.

YOGURT AND COTTAGE CHEESE SAUCE
Version #1

This combination of two important low-fat ingredients is packaged commercially in France, where it's called *fromage blanc.* It's sold on dairy counters in supermarkets, alongside *crème fraîche, petit-suisse,* and yogurt. Office workers in Paris very often have a *fromage blanc* in their brown-bag lunch. This diet food can be made at home in 2 minutes, using the food processor.

1 cup low-fat cottage cheese*
2 tablespoons skim-milk yogurt
few drops lemon juice

First, put in the cottage cheese and yogurt and turn the machine on and off, quickly, to start. Run it for a minute or two until the sauce is completely smooth. Add lemon juice and any seasonings and mix these in at the last.

This spread is good to have with crackers, for hors d'oeuvres. Try seasoning it with a minced clove of garlic, some chopped fresh herbs, or a tablespoon of duxelles (page 135). Or you might want to serve it plain, on crackers, topping it up with an anchovy or (less interestingly) a squirt of anchovy paste, or half an olive.

Yogurt and cottage cheese in this consistency is also suitable for stuffing celery stalks (page 41) and mushroom caps (page 46).

*Low-fat here means 1 or 2 percent butterfat content.

YOGURT AND COTTAGE CHEESE SAUCE
Version #2

Thinner than Version #1, this sauce has a texture reminiscent of sour cream. This second way of presenting yogurt and cottage cheese sauce is for the occasions when you would like a dip — for raw vegetables, for instance. Then you might want to season the sauce with something like curry powder or Chinese Five Spices.

This thinner-textured sauce might also serve as an accompaniment to fish, and then it could be seasoned with horseradish and/or fresh dill. It is a versatile sauce, well worth experimenting with.

 1 cup low-fat cottage cheese*
 4 tablespoons skim-milk yogurt
 few drops lemon juice

Put cheese and yogurt into the food processor and turn the machine on and off quickly until they are well blended. Add lemon juice, and whatever seasonings you have in mind. Chilling the sauce will tend to make it somewhat thicker.

*Again, low-fat here means 1 or 2 percent butterfat content.

YOGURT AND RICOTTA CHEESE SAUCE

This combination is sweeter in taste than the previous sauces, so it's suitable for use with desserts. It somewhat resembles *crème fraîche,* which is a product made of heavy cream and therefore off-limits here.

Yogurt and ricotta sauce needs to be blended in the food processor for 2 minutes, so that every trace of grittiness disappears.

 1 cup skim-milk ricotta cheese
 4 tablespoons skim-milk yogurt
 few drops lemon juice

Blend cheese and yogurt in the food processor for required time, and add lemon juice at the last. Refrigerate until ready to use.

MAYONNAISE
(1½ cups)

Easily made at home in the food processor, mayonnaise is fresh-tasting and delicate, incomparably better than the store-bought kind. It's also healthier, being made of a single whole egg and safflower oil. It keeps well in the refrigerator.

On our Connecticut farm, we raised exotic hens and consequently ate an enormous number of eggs. This conspicuous overconsumption may well have led, in part, to Bud's near-downfall. We had eggs for breakfast, lunch, and supper: in quiches and omelettes, in cream sauces, in desserts such as carrot cake and crème brûlée.

Perhaps I have overreacted, but only three eggs appear in this entire book and then merely as part of dishes to be eaten by at least four people. In mayonnaise, the single whole egg is eaten by many more. Whenever we have occasion to use egg whites, we feed the yolks to the cat.

1 whole egg	black pepper
2 tablespoons lemon juice	herbs, fresh or dried (optional)
1 tablespoon Dijon mustard	tional)
1¼ cups safflower oil	

Put all ingredients except the oil into the food processor. Begin churning and immediately start adding the oil very slowly. As mayonnaise thickens, the machine will make a low roar, which means you can add the rest of the oil and turn it off. Spoon the mayonnaise into a glass jar and refrigerate.

YOGURT MAYONNAISE

I usually mix mayonnaise with an equal portion of skim-milk yogurt. This makes a sauce that is pleasingly tart and highly adaptable to a number of uses.

Perhaps the best of these is as companion to cold chicken or turkey, when a cup of yogurt mayonnaise is laced with a tablespoon of Dijon mustard.

Another use is with cold vegetables served as hors d'oeuvres. A sprinkling of Szechuan pepper or some chopped fresh herbs makes for added interest.

Yogurt mayonnaise is a good spread for cucumber sandwiches, especially when you have some fresh mint at hand and can introduce a few whole leaves.

VINAIGRETTE SALAD DRESSING
(*Serves 4*)

I find the most successful salad dressings are made at the last minute, using only the most elemental ingredients: oil, vinegar, lemon juice. The oil can be a mixture of olive oil and corn oil and the vinegar should be — if possible — sherry wine vinegar. I use only a few drops plus a squirt or two of lemon juice to a tablespoon or so of oil.

It's nice to sprinkle salt and pepper over the chilled lettuce, and a minced clove of garlic never is amiss. Fresh herbs are wonderful, cut over salads.

To make a prepared dressing, for occasions when you are having guests and don't want to leave anything to the last minute, you might include a couple of extras.

2 tablespoons oil (olive and/or corn)	1 teaspoon Dijon mustard
½ teaspoon sherry wine vinegar	1 tablespoon herbs (oregano and/or tarragon)
½ teaspoon lemon juice	1 clove garlic, minced
	black pepper

Mix the dressing in a small glass jar, and shake well. If you are having a salad of mixed vegetables, it is a good idea to let them marinate in the prepared dressing. This means the chilled greens can be added, and the salad tossed together, at the last minute.

BUTTERMILK DRESSING
(*Serves 8*)

This is a grand dressing, especially for a salad into which you are putting a variety of vegetables: raw tomatoes, cucumbers, green peppers, radishes, scallions, red onions, fennel; lightly cooked green beans, peas, broccoli.

1 clove garlic	2 tablespoons mayonnaise
1 teaspoon Dijon mustard	4 tablespoons buttermilk
1 tablespoon safflower oil	black pepper
2 tablespoons skim-milk yogurt	

Mince the garlic and add it to the other ingredients in the blender. Whirl briefly and chill. Use only as much of this dressing as you absolutely need, and save the rest for another occasion. It will keep well for a week, in a tightly closed jar in the refrigerator.

TOMATO SAUCE
(1 cup)

In season, a cupful of heavenly tomato sauce can be quickly made from half a dozen unpeeled whole fresh tomatoes, a minced clove of garlic, and a teaspoon of olive oil. Over moderate heat, cook the tomatoes covered for a couple of minutes. Then, take off the cover, and simmer the pot for about 8 minutes more, giving it an occasional stir. Use immediately, perhaps over a dish of hot rice

But since the season is brief, we usually depend on canned tomatoes for sauce. Imported canned Italian plum tomatoes are excellent; many people prefer them to most store-bought ones.

1 large can Italian plum tomatoes (28 or 35 ounces)	1 teaspoon dried marjoram
	½ teaspoon sugar
1 onion	½ cup red wine
3 garlic cloves	tomato paste — 2 tablespoons or more*
1 bay leaf	
1 teaspoon dried thyme	black pepper

*Tomato paste is useful for thickening, color, and flavor. Most recipes call for a tablespoon of it, and for years — when tomato paste came only in little cans — I

Mince garlic cloves. Cut peeled onion into eighths. Add these to the tomatoes and other seasonings in a large saucepan. Cook uncovered for half an hour, stirring occasionally.

was continually faced with opened cans of the stuff in the refrigerator, which always turned black and had to be thrown away. Now, since the advent of tomato paste in tubes (always available in Italian shops), you can squeeze out a small amount and recap the tube.

PESTO

(1 cup)

Pesto is too good to pass up on a low-fat diet, and I have found that by compromising somewhat with the best Italian recipes (pesto came from Genoa, originally) you still have something totally delicious. I use half their required amounts of oil and cheese. Pesto is not only good on pasta, but on fish and chicken, and it's excellent when used for stuffing broiled tomatoes.

You need lots of fresh basil leaves, so if you like pesto, it pays to grow your own. Make pesto immediately after harvesting the top leaves of your crop; this can be done every few days in good weather. Pesto freezes well, so make plenty of it, but omit the Parmesan, and add it later, at serving time. For a cupful of pesto:

2 cups fresh basil leaves, tightly packed
2 cloves garlic, chopped
3 tablespoons walnuts or pine nuts*

4 tablespoons Parmesan cheese, grated
4 tablespoons oil (olive and corn oil)

Put basil, garlic, nuts, and cheese into the food processor. Whirl them around until they are well mixed and then add the oil, blending until the texture suits you. It will be thick.

*Pine nuts lose half their character (i.e., their crunchy texture) when blended. Since they cost four times as much as walnuts, I tend to use walnuts here and save the pine nuts to use whole in rice, bulgur, and spinach dishes.

To use with pasta, add a couple of tablespoons of the hot cooking water to the pesto and stir it in well. This both heats and thins the sauce. Pour over the pasta in a huge bowl and serve with crusty Italian bread.

Soup

Beautiful soup. We have it for lunch very often, and occasionally a thick soup makes a substantial supper, followed by salad. These soups — hot in winter, cold in summer — are made of beans or peas or fresh vegetables, and are combined with chicken stock, skim-milk yogurt, or buttermilk. The last two are very nearly interchangeable in taste, but the texture of buttermilk is so creamy it's hard to believe it has virtually no fat.

I make my own chicken stock every few days, usually when I am in the kitchen anyway, preparing a meal or making a number of unconnected dishes. Often I get stock by simmering a whole chicken. On other occasions, I draw upon a supply of chicken bones that I accumulate, gradually, in a big plastic bag in the freezer.

Other stock, useful for soup, is made from fish bones. These can be had for the asking from a fish market, where heads, tails, and bones are normally thrown away.

Lobster stock evolves easily when you cover fresh shells with boiling water and cook it energetically until it is reduced to a good, strong broth.

Beef stock is something else again. Not only do we not eat beef, but the kind of work that goes into making traditional beef stock is wildly inappropriate for all but professional French chefs. I use canned beef consommé, hot or cold, and also in buttermilk soup (page 68). We always keep beef consommé in the refrigerator during the summer. It is a very low calorie lunch in itself, topped off with chopped fresh herbs, a squirt of lemon juice, or a scoop of skim-milk yogurt. Tasty and easily accessible, consommé has one disadvantage: it's full of salt, so it should be avoided by anyone concerned about this.

CHICKEN STOCK
(About 1 quart)

We eat chicken all the time in winter and often in summer and seem never to tire of it. A variety of ways of preparing it are described on pages 151–160.

I like to recycle the bones from cooked chicken to make stock. I keep a plastic bag in the freezer in which I collect the bones from roasted, baked, and broiled chickens. When the bag is full, it's time to make stock.

Nothing could be simpler. In a large pot, cover the frozen bones with cold water, bring to a boil, and then reduce the heat, partly cover the pot, and simmer the stock for an hour. Cool, strain, and chill this stock overnight. By morning, a thick layer of fat will have formed on top of the stock, which is very easy to scrape off and throw out. What's left is pure chicken stock. Freeze what you aren't going to use within the next day or two.

With a little more effort, you can have a far more nutritious and tasty stock if you add some vegetables, herbs, and a little wine to the water. To about 8 cups of water, add:

chicken bones	bay leaf
2 chopped onions, unpeeled	thyme, fresh or dried
2 garlic cloves, unpeeled	10 black peppercorns, lightly crushed
2 stalks of celery, halved, with emphasis on leaves	1 tablespoon rice wine vinegar
2 carrots, halved	½ cup dry white wine
parsley stalks, or a few sprigs	

Simmer this stock for 1 hour. Cool, strain, and chill it overnight, then peel the layer of fat off the top.

We still run out of chicken stock, so I keep a few quart-sized cans on hand, one of which is always stored in the refrigerator. When I open this one, the fat will have collected at the surface and can be readily skimmed off.

Incidentally, if, like us, you have a cat, you may find s/he will be most appreciative if you cook the liver, heart, and gizzard that come with every whole chicken and turkey. Collect a few packages in the freezer, as you collect chicken bones. Then, after an hour's simmering in water and a chopping in the food processor, you'll find you have some nutritious and tasty free cat food.

FISH STOCK
(1 quart or more)

Fish stock is produced by boiling up the discarded parts of fish — heads, tails, backbones — that are the detritus of the quickly salable filets. If you happen to be in the fish market when the fileting process is taking place, ask for some of this about-to-be-jettisoned material. If some fresh lobster shells are available, ask for them, too. Alternatively, when you order a whole fish, ask that the trimmings be included with your order.

The only word of caution here is to avoid the rather tasteless carcasses of the oily fish — mackerel or bluefish. Use the bones of fresh cod or haddock for optimum results.

You can make fish stock — a perfect fat-free stock — by adding some herbs and vegetables.

2 pounds fish parts	10 black peppercorns,
3 cups water	lightly crushed
2 stalks celery, with leaves	thyme, fresh or dried
2 onions	parsley stalks or sprigs
bay leaf	

Put everything into a large pot and bring to a boil. Use a long spoon to skim off the foam as it rises to the top. Reduce heat to a simmer, and cook stock, partially covered, for 15 minutes. Strain, cool, and if you're not going to use it immediately, freeze it in one or two small containers until you need it.

BEET SOUP
(Serves 2)

Traditionally, of course, beet soup (or borscht) is a heavy business, made with beef, cabbage, and a dozen other ingredients. It takes hours to cook and is full of fat. Unthinkable on a diet like this one.

However, it occurred to me one day that throwing out the beautiful water in which beets are cooked is a waste, as it could be used as a basis for soup. I reduced and thickened the broth, seasoned it with a sweet-sour combination, and added yogurt to turn the deep red color to palest pink.

3 or more cups beet cooking water	1 teaspoon red wine vinegar
	1 teaspoon sugar
1 onion	1-2 cooked beets (page 120)
1 potato	1 cup skim-milk yogurt

Peel the onion and potato and slice them in the food processor. Add these to the beet broth and cook them, uncovered, over a fairly hot fire. After 15 minutes or so the vegetables should be soft and the broth reduced to 2 cups.

Empty this mixture into the blender, add vinegar, sugar, and one or two beets, quartered. Blend well, chill, and add yogurt at the last minute. Serve cold.

BLACK BEAN SOUP
(Serves 8)

This is a superior soup that makes a meal in itself. Serve it with some French or Italian whole wheat bread and a mixed green salad. A bottle of red wine and some fresh fruit for dessert would complete this feast.

In this book, there are three soups using dried beans that need presoaking before they are cooked; two of these use white beans. Black beans are especially resistant, so they need even more soaking and cooking time. Cover them with plenty of cold water and leave them overnight. Or, if you forget to do this, place them in a saucepan with ample water, and bring to a boil. Simmer them for 2 minutes, remove from heat, and let them soak for an hour before draining them.

1 pound whole black beans, soaked	1 teaspoon ground allspice
10 cups water (or chicken stock, for richer, tastier soup)	¼ teaspoon cayenne (or crushed red) pepper
3 onions	1 pound washed spinach (or 1 box frozen spinach, thawed)
3 cloves garlic	2 tablespoons sherry (or Madeira)
2 carrots	
2 bay leaves	salt, if desired
1 tablespoon dried thyme	lemon slices (or perhaps orange slices) and parsley
1 can tomato paste	sprigs, for garnish
¼ teaspoon ground cloves	

Place the presoaked beans in a large pot and cover them with fresh, cold water or stock. Add peeled and quartered onions, garlic, and carrots, together with bay leaves, spices and the tomato paste. Partially cover the pot and bring it to a boil, lower heat, and simmer until beans are tender. Throw in the spinach and cook for 5 minutes longer. At this point, add salt to taste and sherry or Madeira. Cook the soup for 3 minutes more.

The good, rough texture of this soup recommends it to some people. Personally, I like to cool it slightly and then submit it, little by little, to the blender.

Reheat before serving, and float a slice of lemon or orange on each soup bowl, together with a tiny sprig of parsley.

BUTTERMILK SOUP
(Serves 6)

This is an instant and inspiriting soup. The ingredients are ordinary, but the effect is unusual. This is especially useful for last-minute luncheon guests in summer: you can run it up in 2 minutes.

Incidentally, check to see if you have any salt avoiders at the table, because the consommé is full of it.

2 10-ounce cans beef consommé	1 cup shredded greens: sorrel, spinach, or beet tops
2 cloves garlic	1 quart buttermilk

Mince the garlic and put it in the blender with consommé and greens. When soup is smooth, pour into a pitcher and stir in buttermilk. Serve with warmed pita bread.

CARROT SOUP
(Serves 4)

Cream of carrot soup is a French specialty that I used to adore. It is thickened with egg yolks and heavy cream, and now I find all that richness faintly revolting. In this version of carrot soup, potato provides the thickening. Cumin and red pepper give pungency to the taste of the carrots.

1½ pounds carrots	1 teaspoon ground cumin (more or less)
1 stalk celery	½ teaspoon crushed red pepper
1 onion	
1 potato	lots of chopped parsley for garnish
6 cups chicken stock	
1 teaspoon tomato paste	

Peel the onion and potato, and grate them, together with the carrots and celery, in the food processor. Simmer them for 20 minutes or so in chicken stock and seasonings. Blend and serve very hot, topped with chopped parsley. Dark pumpernickel bread goes well with this soup, as does a mixed green salad.

CORN CHOWDER
(Serves 4)

This is particularly simple if you have leftover ears of cooked corn. If this shouldn't be the case, start out fresh with four ears of corn and steam them (see page 130).

4 ears steamed corn	pepper
2 cloves garlic, minced	salt, to taste
1 quart milk*	

Heat the quart of milk in a saucepan.
Scrape the kernels off the ears of steamed corn.
In the blender, combine corn and garlic together with 1 cup of the warm milk. When they are thoroughly integrated, pour this mixture into the remaining milk on the stove. Heat well, and serve piping hot.

*This chowder, as well as the fish chowder on page 70, is greatly improved if you use 99 percent fat-free milk instead of the regular skim milk. You'll find that the chowder tastes unusually rich and creamy.

CUCUMBER SOUP
(Serves 8)

This summer soup is thin and tangy with slices of cucumber floating about in it.

2 English cucumbers (or 6 small local ones)	6 cups skim-milk yogurt (or buttermilk)
3 cloves garlic	pepper
1 quart chicken stock	salt, to taste

Mince garlic cloves. Cut the cucumbers in half, vertically, then thinly slice them in the food processor.

In large bowl or pitcher, stir together the chicken stock and yogurt. Season this mixture. Add garlic and cucumbers to soup and serve icy cold.

ESCAROLE AND WHITE BEAN SOUP
(Serves 8)

This is a lovely, sturdy soup: its flavor depends on escarole, a somewhat bitter-tasting Italian lettuce. When the escarole is combined with rather bland white beans, the result is interesting. These beans need to be presoaked before cooking. See page 82 for directions.

2 cups white beans*	2–3 tablespoons Tamari
1 pound escarole	sauce
8 cups chicken stock	pepper
3 cloves garlic, minced	salt, to taste
oregano, fresh or dried	

Drain the presoaked beans and rinse them in cold water. Cover them with chicken stock and add the garlic. Cook for ½ hour or so, partially covered.

Add whole, washed escarole leaves and seasonings and cook soup for another 15 minutes or so. Taste for flavor and adjust the seasonings.

*These white beans might be Great Northern beans, or white kidney beans (cannellini) found in Italian shops.

FISH CHOWDER
(Serves 6 to 8)

A fine filling soup, based on the fish stock described on pages 65–66, fish chowder can provide a main course for a summer dinner party. Have a huge green salad, with bright vegetables, and some dark bread as a second course. For dessert: cut-up summer fruits and berries in red wine.

4 potatoes	juice of 1 lemon
4 onions	handful fresh dill (or other
2 cloves garlic	herb)
3 cups water	3 pounds haddock
4 cups fish stock (see page	salt, to taste
65)	2 cups milk*
fresh-ground pepper	fresh parsley, for garnish

Peel potatoes, onions, and garlic and slice them in the food processor. Simmer these in water until tender (20 minutes or so). Add fish stock, pepper, lemon juice, and dill to pot and simmer for 10 minutes more.

Cut haddock into chunks and add to soup, cooking for no more than 5 minutes. Add salt, to taste. During this time, warm the milk and add it at the last moment. Sprinkle fresh parsley over the top and serve with warmed crackers.

*This chowder, as well as the corn chowder on page 69, is greatly improved if you use 99 percent fat-free milk instead of the regular skim milk. You'll find that the chowder tastes unusually rich and creamy.

GAZPACHO
(Serves 4)

This fine summer soup, made from fresh tomatoes, is very easy to accomplish in the blender. Gazpacho was originally a Spanish soup. The variations on it are nearly endless, but here is a basic structure:

4–5 tomatoes, peeled	½ teaspoon crushed red pep-
1 native cucumber	per
2 cloves garlic, minced	½ teaspoon coriander seeds,
2 tablespoons olive oil	crushed
1 tablespoon wine vinegar	1 cup chicken stock

Garnishes

chopped scallions	stoned black olives
sliced radishes	chopped chives

Peel tomatoes after immersing them in boiling water for 10 seconds, when the skin will virtually fall off by itself. Cut tomatoes into quarters. Cut the unpeeled cucumber into chunks, and put these vegetables into the blender. Add the other ingredients and mix thoroughly. Chill.

It's nice to serve this soup with tiny bowls of garnishes, placed at the center of the table so people can help themselves.

LENTIL SOUP
(Serves 6)

Lentil and green split pea soups (page 76) are the only two bean soups that can be made on the spur of the moment, without the beans having been soaked. This is a tremendous advantage.

I prefer lentil soup with the beans whole, and split pea soup in a puréed state. So although the differences in preparation are minimal, I offer separate recipes. The seasoning here is cribbed directly from Simon and Garfunkel.

1 pound lentils	1 large onion
8 cups water	2 cloves garlic
2 stalks celery with leaves	1 bay leaf
1 tablespoon mild red wine vinegar	cayenne pepper
	salt, to taste
generous amounts of: parsley	
sage	
rosemary	
thyme	

Rinse the lentils under cold, running water, picking them over to disclose any small stones that might have been included. Peel and then chop the vegetables in the food processor and combine with lentils, water, and seasonings. Simmer, partially covered, for ½ hour or so, until lentils are tender. Taste and adjust seasonings until soup is exactly right.

Toasted whole-grain bread or pita bread, a green salad, and voilà — supper, or lunch, as the case may be.

MINT SOUP
(Serves 6)

A summertime version of split pea soup, this soup is especially suitable for people with easy access to a mint patch.

1 pound dried green split peas	few grains cayenne pepper
7 cups chicken stock	1 cup skim-milk yogurt
1 cup fresh mint leaves	mint leaves for garnish

Wash peas under cold, running water and search for stones.

Combine peas, mint, and chicken stock in a large saucepan and bring to a boil. Lower heat, cover, and simmer for ½ hour.

Cool the soup slightly and then whirl in blender. Add cayenne pepper. Chill.

Just before serving, add yogurt, stirring it in well. Garnish each soup bowl with a fresh mint leaf.

ONION SOUP
(Serves 2)

Onion soup makes a good supper on a cold winter night. The old French custom of baking the soup in separate bowls is now frowned on as being somewhat dangerous and messy. Gruyère cheese is the preferred topping for this soup, but since we use it for nothing else, we substitute Parmesan.

2 cups sliced onions	1 tablespoon brandy
1 tablespoon corn oil	2 slices French bread
2 cans beef consommé	2 tablespoons fresh-grated
¾ cup white wine	Parmesan cheese

Heat up the consommé and wine in a saucepan.

In food processor, slice onions. In nonstick pan, heat the oil and sauté the onions lightly. Add them to the hot consommé mixture and simmer, covered, for ½ hour or more. Add brandy for the last few minutes.

Place the bread, covered with the cheese, in toaster (or regular) oven. Bake these until the bread is crisp and the cheese is melted. Place this toast in the bottom of two bowls, and pour the hot soup over them. Serve at once.

PROVENÇAL SOUP
(Serves 8)

This is *soupe au pistou,* a certain amount of trouble but worth every minute. Make it at the end of summer, when fresh string beans and fresh basil are abundant, and serve it at a feast. The night before, cover 1 cup dried white beans (Great Northern, preferably) with cold water to soak for 8 hours. If you should forget to do this, soften the beans by the quick method described on page 82. They will double in bulk.

Soup

5 carrots	2 cups fresh string beans
2 large potatoes	½ cup small-sized pasta
3 onions	1 slice bread, crumbled
2 cups soaked white beans	pepper
3 quarts water	salt, to taste

Peel the root vegetables (carrots, potatoes, and onions) and slice them in the food processor. You should have about 2 cups of each.

Drain the soaked white beans and rinse them with fresh water. Cook these, together with the root vegetables, in three quarts of water, for ½ hour over medium heat, covered.

Cut the string beans into 1-inch pieces, and add them, together with the crumbled slice of bread and the pasta, to the soup. Cook for 15 minutes more, or until the green beans are right. Season with pepper and salt, to taste.

In food processor, prepare the pistou (which is like pesto, except that it uses tomato paste instead of pine nuts).

Pistou

4 cloves garlic	¼ cup fresh-grated Parmesan cheese
4 tablespoons tomato paste	
½ cup fresh basil leaves, tightly packed	4 tablespoons oil (partly olive oil)

When this sauce is well blended, place it in the bottom of a soup tureen. Add 1 cup hot soup and stir well. Then add the remainder of the hot soup and serve immediately. Have a big, warm loaf of French or Italian bread to go with it.

SPLIT PEA SOUP
(Serves 6)

We used to think that a ham bone was an essential ingredient in either lentil or split pea soup. For some reason, this soup was supposed to cook for 3 hours, and when it was done it was greasy and generally difficult to manage.

Split pea soup in the new mode cooks in ½ hour and contains no fat at all.

2 cups dried green split peas	2 stalks celery, with leaves
8 cups water	3 tablespoons Tamari sauce
2 carrots	1 teaspoon Szechuan pepper
2 onions	oregano, fresh or dried
2 garlic cloves	

Rinse peas in cold water, and place them in a large pot with the water. Peel and coarsely chop the garlic and vegetables and toss them in, too. Simmer this brew, partly covered, for ½ hour or so.

For additional flavor, heat the Szechuan peppercorns in a nonstick pan, until they give off a wonderful aroma. Add pepper, oregano, and Tamari sauce to the soup and keep tasting it until you feel the flavor is exactly right. Purée in blender. If you're not serving it right away, reheat and serve soup piping hot with a warmed loaf of fresh sourdough bread.

SWEET POTATO SOUP
(Serves 4)

I like this soup both for its color and for its flavor. It can be a meal in itself.

4 sweet potatoes	¼ teaspoon ground cloves
3 cups chicken stock	¼ teaspoon ground nutmeg
juice of ½ orange	1 cup buttermilk
juice of ½ lemon	yogurt for garnish
few grains cayenne pepper	

Steam the sweet potatoes until they are soft and then peel them — the skins will slip off quite easily. Cut them into pieces and purée them in the blender with the fruit juices, spices, and half the chicken stock.

Add this purée to the rest of the chicken stock in a saucepan over medium heat and mix thoroughly. At the very last add the buttermilk and continue cooking until soup is piping hot. Then serve immediately, with a trail of yogurt across the top.

TOMATO SOUP
(Serves 6)

This is a spicy soup, made in the blender and served cold. Because it uses tomato juice instead of fresh tomatoes, it's a good recipe for those occasions when a decent tomato is impossible to find.

3 cups tomato juice	½ teaspoon coriander
2 tablespoons tomato paste	pepper
½ red onion, quartered	2 cups yogurt
1 teaspoon curry powder	chopped parsley
½ teaspoon cumin	

Put all ingredients except yogurt and parsley into the blender and whirl. Add yogurt and mix well. Chill soup and sprinkle with chopped parsley just before serving.

ZUCCHINI SOUP
(Serves 4)

This quick and easy summer soup, served cold, is equally good in winter, served hot.

3 medium zucchini squash
1 large onion
4 cups chicken stock

2 teaspoons Madras curry
    powder
pepper

Use the grating disk on the food processor to prepare the squash and onion. Add them, with seasonings, to the chicken stock and simmer, covered, for 20 minutes.

Peas, Beans, and Whole Grains

These foods are truly the centerpiece of a low-fat way of life. They are eaten at every meal, or at a minimum of two meals a day, beginning with the morning cereal, hot or cold; continuing through lunch with bread or toast and a bean soup; and concluding with dinner, when rice, bulgur, pasta, or grains such as cornmeal or grits are served, with or without accompanying fish or chicken.

We used to think these foods made us fat — and they were the first thing sacrificed to a diet plan. But now it's known these foods contain vital fibers, are very high in protein, and one could be perfectly well fed if one ate just these foods together with a few fresh vegetables and some fruit.

Actually, it was the butter slathered on bread and toast, the sugar and cream on cereal, that was fattening. Beans and whole grains can be beautifully seasoned with garlic, shallots, herbs, and chicken stock, and I think you'll find these foods — as we do — truly satisfying. They give one a sense of being comfortably full after eating, but never stuffed. Because the fiber attracts fluids to itself, the digestive system is charged with energy and human plumbing works like a charm.

The presence of a "significant other" is central to a consideration of beans and whole grains. They need each other. Alone, they have — like people — limited power, but combined with an appropriate partner, they burgeon with energy. This is easy to understand if you reflect on beans and rice, the traditional and instinctively sound food of many developing countries.

There are similar combinations in this book: for instance, lentils are combined with bulgur and black-eyed peas with rice. But there are other, less obvious, duos because, as it happens, dairy products are also satisfactory complements for both beans and whole grains. So we have yogurt with black beans and mozzarella with cornmeal. Seeds and nuts, as well as shoyu Tamari sauce (made of soybeans and cracked wheat), quietly energize whatever legume or whole-grain dish they become part of.

It's interesting to note how this has worked out over the years in every country. In the Middle East, hummous (a combination of sesame seeds and chick-peas) is a staple. In Mexico, cornmeal tortillas are served in tandem with pinto beans. In the United States, children enjoy peanut butter sandwiches without being aware of the fact that they're doing just the right thing.

All dried beans, except for lentils and split peas, need to be presoaked to shorten their cooking time. This is easy. Wash the beans under cold running water in a strainer, and then place them in a bowl, covered with plenty of cold water. Leave them, uncovered, on the kitchen counter for 8 hours or so; this could be either all day or overnight. Their cooking time, after this soaking, is usually about ½ hour — black beans and black-eyed peas take longer.

There is another method of presoaking that is quicker. It takes only a little over an hour, but it requires attention, which I'm reluctant to give for something so mundane. However, it's an expedient scheme for those times when you've forgotten to plan ahead.

Cover the beans with cold water in a saucepan, and bring to a boil. Simmer them for 2 minutes. Turn off heat and let them soak for 1 hour. Drain and cook. I think that's quite a lot of trouble, whereas the first method is a cinch.

BLACK-EYED PEAS AND RICE
(Serves 8)

Sturdy and succulent, this southern classic is traditionally made with pork fat. Naturally, we turn to herbs and garlic for flavoring. If you add some cooked chicken to this dish, it is very good fare indeed.

1 pound black-eyed peas
6 cups water
1 onion, stuck with 2 cloves
2 gloves garlic, peeled, cut
   in half
1 bay leaf

1-2 tablespoons dried thyme
   (or twice as much fresh
   thyme)
1 cup rice
1 cup cooked chicken (op-
   tional)

Soak the peas for 8 or 10 hours in cold water (or use quick method described on page 82). Drain and cover with fresh water.

Add onion, garlic, bay leaf, and thyme, and bring pot to boil. Then reduce heat and simmer, covered, for 45 minutes or even more, until the peas are tender but not mushy. Drain the peas.

While you are simmering the peas, prepare the rice following the directions on page 111. When rice has cooked, leave it on the stove, covered; it will retain its heat.

As liaison for the peas and rice, you will need a sauce rich with garlic and shallots, based on chicken stock.

Sauce

1 onion
2 shallots
1 garlic clove
2 tablespoons corn oil
1 cup (or more) chicken
   stock

marjoram or oregano
fresh parsley
pepper
salt, to taste

Chop the vegetables and herbs in the food processor. Then sauté them briefly in the oil in a nonstick pan. Scoop them out and mix them into the cooked peas. Add the rice (and cooked chicken chunks, if you are using them), pepper, and salt. Pour on stock so that dish is full of moisture but not soggy. Bake this concoction in a large dish, in a moderate (350°) oven for about ½ hour. Add more stock, if you feel it's necessary.

Serve with a deliberately colorful salad: tomatoes, red pepper, radishes, and red onions chopped into a big bowl of lettuce. With a loaf of French bread and a bottle of red wine, you have an excellent meal. A good dessert might be prunes with kumquats (page 197).

CHICK-PEAS

A bowl of chick-peas, at room temperature, dressed with vinaigrette and some garlic, makes a fine adjunct to broiled fish and sliced tomatoes.

Or, you might want to serve them as a main dish, in which case you could add some cooked rice and/or chicken. Then spinach salad with oranges (page 148) might be an appropriate complement.

Chick-peas need to be soaked in cold water for 8 hours, either all day or overnight. (For fast, alternative method, see page 82). Drain soaked peas, cover with fresh water, and simmer them for half an hour or so. They should be tender, but still firm.

If you cook a whole pound of chick-peas, you'll have enough for the salad (page 85) as well as a batch of hummous (page 43). This dip keeps well in the refrigerator and will give you an instant spread for hors d'oeuvres or filling for pita bread anytime you need it. If you decide to make hummous, save a cup of the cooking water from the chick-peas for the dip: it contains nutrients, provides moisture, and adds flavor, too.

CHICK-PEA SALAD
(Serves 4)

Here is a simple way to present chick-peas. Have some toasted pita bread and sliced tomatoes to go with them.

2 cups cooked chick-peas	2 tablespoons oil (partly
1 clove garlic	olive oil)
½ red onion	few drops red wine vinegar
parsley	pepper
dill (or some other herb)	salt, to taste

In food processor, chop garlic, onion, parsley, and dill (or whatever herb you have decided on). Add this mixture to bowl of chick peas and mix well. Add oil, vinegar, pepper, and salt, to taste. Stir well and chill.

GREAT NORTHERN BEANS
(Serves 8)

These beans are very like those used in France to make cassoulet, that succulent traditional dish of Toulouse that combines beans with roast duck and braised lamb. They are so good that I like to have them as a main dish. With them goes whole wheat bread and a richly varied salad: a Greek salad (page 146) would be ideal.

For some reason, Great Northern beans aren't always easy to find (but horrid little navy beans and tasteless limas are everywhere). When you see some, pick up a few pounds. Like all dried beans, they have a long shelf life.

These beans need to be presoaked, either overnight, or by the quick method described on page 82. After draining them, cover with fresh water and bring to a boil. Reduce heat, partially cover, and simmer them for ½ hour until tender, but pleasantly firm. For 1 pound cooked beans, make a sauce:

3 tablespoons oil	1 red onion, skinned
few drops mild red wine vinegar	chopped fresh herbs (tarragon or marjoram)
1 teaspoon lemon juice	a drop of Tamari sauce
3 cloves garlic, minced	fresh-ground black pepper
1 teaspoon Dijon mustard	salt, to taste

Thinly slice the red onion in the food processor, and place in a small bowl with the other ingredients. When well mixed (and tasted to see if salt is needed), pour over beans. Serve at room temperature.

ITALIAN BEANS AND TUNA
(Serves 4)

This dish, made with canned foods, might seem out of place in this fresh-food cookbook. But it's useful for a rainy night, when you need to exploit the kitchen shelves and you're tired of pasta.

With a green salad, and some dark bread, you have a complete meal.

1 16-ounce can cannellini*	3 tablespoons lemon juice
1 7-ounce can solid white tuna packed in water	2 scallions
3 tablespoons oil (partly olive)	parsley, chopped
	pepper
	salt, if desired

Drain and rinse in cold water both beans and tuna. Chill the tuna.

In a large salad bowl, place oil and lemon juice. Add beans and blend well. Let this mixture rest for an hour on the kitchen counter.

Chop the scallions, top and bottom, with a sharp knife.

*Cannellini are Italian white kidney beans, closely related to Great Northern beans, and also very good. They can always be found in Italian shops.

Chop the parsley, if you don't already have a jarful in the refrigerator (see page 12).

Just before serving, add the tuna, scallions, and parsley to the beans, check for seasonings, and mix well.

CURRIED BLACK BEANS
(*Serves 8*)

For some reason, these beans are quite glamorous; perhaps it's their color. You need not worry about serving them at a supper party: they make a hit. Serve them with rice and a big bowl of yogurt. Italian bread and a salad composed of a variety of lettuces and vegetables are a good follow-up. Then a luscious dessert would complete this feast.

The only drawback here is presoaking and cooking time. The beans need all-night soaking and anywhere from 1½ to 2 hours of slow simmering to bring them to proper tenderness. They are an exception that, I hope, proves the rule in this book where almost everything is very quickly prepared, i.e., fast. They are appropriately low in fat, and very easy to cook.

1 pound presoaked black beans	3 tablespoons Madras curry powder
6 cups chicken stock	1 teaspoon lemon juice (or lime juice)
handful fresh parsley (American or Chinese)	1 tablespoon red wine vinegar
2-3 large onions	
3-4 garlic cloves	1 cup (or more) residual cooking stock
3 tablespoons corn or safflower oil	

Cover the beans with chicken stock, bring them to a boil, reduce the heat, cover the pot, and simmer them for 1½ to 2 hours: they should be both tender and firm.

In the food processor, chop the parsley and then empty the container into a bowl. Chop the onions and garlic.

When beans are cooked, drain the considerable residue of chicken stock into a saucepan or other container and save this: you may well need it to lend added moisture to this dish (a cup or so is usually needed). The rest you could use to make black bean soup out of any leftover beans.

Heat the oil in a nonstick pan and sauté the chopped onions and garlic. Sprinkle on the curry powder and stir in the lemon or lime juice, the vinegar, and a cupful of the residual stock. Cook this mixture for 10 minutes, and pour over the hot beans. Just before serving, scatter the parsley over the beans and lightly mix it in.

TOFU
(Serves 4)

Tofu, called bean curd by the Chinese, is a solid white cake made of pressed soybeans, and therefore super-rich in protein. Freshly made tofu has a delicate texture and a subtle, rather pleasing taste, but it is almost impossible to find except in special East Asian restaurants where it's created on the premises.

For home consumption, you can buy tofu in sealed 1-pound packages or in smaller chunks, sold in plastic baskets floating in water. Once opened, tofu should be kept covered with fresh water. Since commercial tofu is without taste, it needs to be highly seasoned. Vegetarians like to add bits of it to soups or salads, but I am wary of tasteless additives. The following sauce, whipped up in minutes, makes tofu just as satisfying and quick a dish as scrambled eggs used to be when we ate a "normal" diet. Toasted pita bread and some crisp watercress make amiable companions for tofu.

Sauce for 1 Pound of Tofu

1 pound tofu
2 garlic cloves
2 slices gingerroot, peeled
1 scallion, green and white
   parts
1 small zucchini squash

1 teaspoon Szechuan pepper
1 tablespoon sesame oil
1 tablespoon (or more) Tamari sauce
fresh Chinese parsley

Press the water out of the tofu, by squeezing it in the corner of a clean dish towel. Chop it into cubes.

Mince garlic and gingerroot in the food processor. Using a knife, slice the zucchini and scallion into tiny pieces. Sauté all these and the Szechuan pepper in the oil in a nonstick pan. Add tofu and Tamari sauce, and stir until the tofu is heated. Sprinkle parsley over all, and serve at once.

LENTILS
(Serves 4)

These tiny brown beans need no soaking. They are good served at room temperature. They also make good soup (page 72) and combine well with bulgur (page 92). Also, lentils make an interesting stuffing for toasted pita bread pockets, together with a few alfalfa sprouts and some sliced tomato.

For a main dish to serve with a bowl of fresh, skim-milk yogurt and a mixed green salad, lentils are simplicity itself.

1 cup lentils   2½ cups chicken stock

Rinse the beans under cold running water before putting them into an enamel-lined pot with the stock. Simmer them gently, partly covered, for ½ hour—the liquid should be completely absorbed.

Season them with:

1 small onion	1-2 teaspoons red wine vin-
2 cloves garlic	egar
fresh parsley, American or	fresh-ground pepper
Chinese	salt, to taste
2 tablespoons corn oil	

In food processor, chop onion, garlic, and parsley together. Add these to cooked lentils. Pour over them oil, vinegar, and other seasonings and mix well.

Lentils, at room temperature, will be ready when you are. They are also splendid served hot.

BULGUR
(Serves 8)

Bulgur is one of the major discoveries in my search for delicious, low-fat food. It is precooked cracked wheat, so it needs virtually no cooking. It is nutty in flavor, and can be served hot, cold, or at room temperature. It can be a main dish, when accompanied by a bowl of fresh skim-milk yogurt. With either chicken or fish, it makes a good substitute for the more usual rice. It can be used for stuffing baked tomatoes and is a splendid addition to salad.

For a main dish:

2 cups bulgur
boiling water to cover
a handful of currants (optional)

Put the bulgur in a bowl and pour over it precisely enough boiling water to cover it. In ½ hour the water will be absorbed.

For bulgur at room temperature, add the following:

3 tablespoons corn oil
salt, to taste
2 chopped scallions, both white and green parts

With a fork, stir the bulgur until it is fluffy. Add oil and salt, and top off with the chopped scallions.

If, on the other hand, you'd like the bulgur hot, you have two choices. One is to reheat the above mix in a double boiler.

The second method is as follows:

1 whole onion
2–3 tablespoons corn oil
salt, to taste

Chop the peeled onion in the food processor. Sauté it lightly in the oil in a nonstick saucepan. Add the bulgur, stir together. Finally, salt to taste.

TABBOULEH
(Serves 6)

A Middle Eastern dish, tabbouleh is characterized by the strong flavors of fresh mint and parsley. Serve it during the summer months when these herbs are abundant, and you want a light but filling dish for lunch or supper.

Yogurt with cucumbers (see page 132) would go well with it, and perform the additional service of completing the protein.

2 cups previously cooked
  bulgur (page 90)
1–2 peeled, chopped tomatoes*
2–3 chopped scallions
3–4 chopped mushrooms
1 cup minced parsley

½ cup chopped fresh mint
1–3 tablespoons oil (partly
  olive oil)
4 tablespoons lemon juice
black pepper
salt, if desired

Mix all these ingredients together and serve chilled or at room temperature.

*Tomatoes can be easily peeled if they are submerged for 10 seconds in boiling water. The skin then comes off in big strips.

BULGUR PILAF
(Serves 4)

This is a wonderful dish, with which you might serve fresh green peas or string beans, some baked tomatoes or a salad, followed by a dessert made of ricotta cheese.

1 onion	2 tablespoons chopped pars-
1 tablespoon corn or saf-	ley
flower oil	2 tablespoons pine nuts
1 cup bulgur*	
2 cups chicken stock	

Chop the onion in the food processor, and then sauté these pieces in the oil in a nonstick pan. As the onion becomes golden, add the bulgur. Stir until the grains are coated, and then add the stock.

Cook this, covered, for 15 minutes. By this time all the moisture should be absorbed.

Mix in parsley and pine nuts and serve hot.

*Kasha (buckwheat groats) may be used instead of the bulgur in this recipe. The grains are larger, the taste more aggressive. I greatly prefer the bulgur, but this is a personal bias.

BULGUR AND LENTILS
(Serves 8)

This is a traditional peasant dish from the Middle East, where beans and grains are naturally intertwined, providing perfect nutrition. It is delicious on a very cold winter Sunday, for a lunch when you have guests. Follow the bean dish with a light salad — watercress and Belgian endive would be ideal. For dessert: apple crisp (page 188).

2 cups lentils	pepper
8 cups water	salt, to taste
1 cup bulgur	grating of fresh nutmeg
1 onion	
1 tablespoon corn or saf-	
flower oil	

Rinse lentils, cover with water, and bring to a boil. Reduce heat and simmer uncovered for 15 minutes. Add bulgur and cook for another 15 minutes. Stir occasionally, until all liquid is absorbed. Season with pepper. Salt to taste.

In food processor, chop the onion. Heat oil in a nonstick pan and sauté the onion lightly. Add to lentils, together with fresh nutmeg. Serve hot.

CORNMEAL
(Serves 2)

I am quite addicted to cornmeal, and have been since infancy. I find it unutterably delicious, a comfort to body and spirit. It makes for an ideal meal on a night when you are hungry, but too tired to cook. However, it's also excellent as a side dish for a dinner party, when you are having chicken or fish, and one or two bright-colored vegetables.* People are intrigued by it, wonder what it is.

I am embarrassed by the old-time American name for this dish ("cornmeal mush"), but it would be inaccurate and pretentious to call it polenta, because polenta it isn't. The Italians chill their mush and cut it into squares; these are fried in olive oil and served with tomato sauce.

For a simple supper for two people:

*Much the same can be said for hominy grits as a comforting cereal food to eat on an off night. And grits also go beautifully with roast chicken or turkey at a party.
Easier to cook than cornmeal, grits can be added dry to boiling water, and they cook in 10 minutes. The proportions are 1 part cereal to 5 parts water. If you decide not to use ham, you'll need salt for seasoning.

½ cup cornmeal	1 or 2 slices baked ham
¼ cup cold water	parsley
2 cups boiling water	¼ teaspoon cayenne pepper
1 1-ounce chunk mozzarella cheese	1 tablespoon Parmesan cheese (optional)

First, mix the cornmeal with ¼ cup of cold water, stirring with a fork until it is perfectly free of lumps. Then, using the top of a double boiler, bring 2 cups of water to a boil over direct heat, and add the cornmeal mix to the boiling water. Stir until the cereal is all thick and smooth. Then return the top of the double boiler to its companion piece, and let the cornmeal cook over simmering water for 20 or 25 minutes.

While this is going on, chop the mozzarella, the ham, and some parsley together in the food processor. (Plain mozzarella is good, smoked is heavenly.) When cornmeal is cooked, add these ingredients and then stir in a little cayenne and a tablespoon or so of Parmesan cheese.

PANCAKES STUFFED WITH HAM AND MUSHROOMS
(Serves 4)

This is a superb main dish for lunch or supper, most of which can be prepared ahead of time. It substitutes for crêpes, which are off-limits, being made almost entirely of eggs.

1 cup homemade pancake mix (page 34)
1 egg
1½ cups buttermilk

Combine these ingredients in a bowl, stirring gently with a fork, but leaving the mixture somewhat lumpy. (Too much smoothness makes for heavy pancakes.)

Heat a large nonstick pan and make, one at a time, four

large pancakes, turning them to brown both sides. Set pancakes aside, covered with a dish towel, to be reheated in the oven later.

Put together the stuffing:

2–3 mushrooms	1 tablespoon marjoram
2 slices cooked ham*	1 tablespoon dry vermouth
2 cloves garlic	1 cup skim-milk yogurt
2 shallots	additional yogurt for
1 tablespoon minced parsley	garnish

In the food processor, chop the ham or chicken, herbs, and mushrooms. Combine all these in a bowl, and add yogurt and vermouth. Chill if you're not going to use right away.

Just before the meal, preheat the oven to 375°. In a small nonstick saucepan, heat up the stuffing mixture. Spread the pancakes out on the kitchen counter and place a quarter of the mixture in the center of each. Roll them up and place them on a flat, ovenproof platter. Bake for 15 minutes, and serve with a trail of yogurt across the top of each pancake.

*You may prefer to use ½ cup cooked chicken instead.

WHOLE WHEAT BREAD

The good news is that on a low-fat diet you can eat bread constantly without getting fat. What you can't eat is the butter that we all — alas — have got so used to putting on it. We need to remind ourselves of our gourmet models, the French, who always eat their bread unbuttered.

As I mentioned in my Introduction, my husband has taken up bread making. What a boon this is. His best product — French bread — is unfortunately too time-consuming for this cookbook: it's low, but it's not fast. He needs to be near it over a period of 6 or 8 hours.

But his second-best bread is made in less than 2 hours and it's superb. It's a round loaf, half whole wheat, crusty, and full of flavor. It keeps indefinitely in the refrigerator, and is best eaten the day after it's made, when it should be sliced and toasted.

There are, however, two caveats: one is that the food processor, used in almost every recipe in this book, can't be used here. Instead, an electric mixer does the work of kneading the first time around. The second kneading must be done by hand; this is somewhat arduous. But if you are an amateur, you will apparently find this a very easy bread to begin on.

2 cups lukewarm water	2 tablespoons sugar
2 tablespoons granular yeast*	2 tablespoons margarine
2 garlic cloves	2 teaspoons salt
⅓ cup nonfat dry milk	2 cups white flour
	2 cups whole wheat flour

Topping

1 white of egg, mixed with
1 tablespoon water
¼ cup sesame seeds

Dissolve yeast in warm water. Mince garlic.

Put these into a large bowl, and add dry milk, sugar, margarine, salt, and the 2 cups of white flour. With electric beater set at lowest speed, beat this mixture for 2 minutes.

Sprinkle in the 2 cups of whole wheat flour. Before beginning to knead the dough, wet your hands to prevent their sticking. Knead the dough for 2 minutes. Place in a bowl covered with a damp dish towel, and let dough rise for 40 minutes. (Set timer.) It will double in bulk.

Preheat oven to 375°. Knead the dough again, for 2 more minutes. Grease a straight-sided container — a saucepan or soufflé dish will do — and pour batter in.

*The best yeast is found in health-food stores.

Brush top of loaf with egg white and water beaten together, and sprinkle sesame seeds over all. Bake for 1 hour.

When cooled, remove bread from baking dish, wrap it in a plastic bag, and put it in the refrigerator until the following day.

Pasta

Making pasta at home is a tiresome process, but as basic to Italian chefs as beef stock is to French chefs. What a relief we don't have to do it. Since homemade pasta (as well as that sold fresh or frozen in shops) is made of flour and eggs, for the purposes of this diet, it's out.

We must confine ourselves to the many variations of pasta sizes and designs that are sold in boxes. The best is imported from Italy, but Ronzoni is an excellent American pasta. Spaghetti and macaroni are made of flour and water, so they keep well on a grocery or kitchen shelf. As everyone knows, pasta makes wonderful instant food.

Cooking pasta well requires a certain amount of concentration so you are sure not to overcook it. Fill a big pot with 4 quarts of water, and add 1 tablespoon of safflower oil to keep the pasta from sticking. Use 1 pound of pasta for 4 generous servings; use ¾ pound for lower expectations. Cover the pot, and when water comes to a hard boil, drop the pasta in slowly and stir it until the boiling resumes. Then, without lowering the heat, cook it uncovered.

If you're cooking slim spaghetti, begin tasting for doneness after 5 minutes. If you're having ziti, shells, or spirals, 10 minutes is time enough before you begin the tasting process. The pasta is ready when it is still firm, but not so underdone that you get a taste of flour.

During the cooking process, heat the oven to 300°, and warm the serving bowl and plates. Hot pasta chills quickly, and warm plates are a pleasant way to retard this process.

Dump the cooked pasta into a colander in the kitchen sink, but leave enough water in it so it isn't dry. Mix quickly with whatever sauce you've prepared, and whisk pasta to the table.

A number of suggested sauces for pasta follow, but the possibilities are endless. Almost everything combines well with this most satisfactory of foods.

Your choice of oil to use in pasta sauces may be simply corn oil, or perhaps corn oil mixed with a little olive oil, or even all olive oil. It's nice to vary this; there is no absolute rule.

In buying pasta, it's fun to get a variety of shapes and sizes. I like corkscrew-shaped pasta a lot; it's called Rotelle by the Ronzoni company, and Fusilli by DeCecco. For simplicity's sake, I call them both spirals. I also like tiny forms of pasta — orzo and tubettini — as a pleasant variation.

PASTA WITH OIL AND CHEESE
(Serves 2)

The quickest, easiest and commonest sauce for pasta is olive oil and fresh-grated Parmesan cheese.* This can be improved, to my mind, by adding garlic, and marjoram. This sauce is perfect with the slimmest of spaghettis, which is also the fastest cooking.

For two people, prepare ½ pound of pasta, cooking it in 4 quarts of water. For the sauce you need:

2 tablespoons oil (1 each of olive and corn oil)	pepper
	salt, to taste
2 cloves garlic, minced	1 or 2 tablespoons grated
2 tablespoons dried marjoram	Parmesan

*An equally simple — and uncooked — sauce, pesto, is described on page 58.

Just before the pasta is done, heat the oil in a nonst'
Add minced garlic, marjoram, pepper, and salt, to taste. ๖ι..
quickly, so nothing burns. Mix this sauce into hot pasta and
sprinkle with fresh-grated Parmesan.

PASTA PRIMAVERA
(Serves 4)

This is a fancy name for a dish that provides a good way to
use up leftovers. If you have a cup of peas or a dish of broccoli from the night before, this is a fine way to use it up. But
don't use leftover vegetables if they have been around any
longer than that; instead, consider soup.

This dish of pasta with vegetables is colorful and good-
looking. Make it with shells or spirals, preferably.

Put 4 quarts of water on to boil for 1 pound of pasta, and
begin making the sauce.

1-2 tomatoes	3 tablespoons corn oil
1 small zucchini	1 cup cooked peas (or
2 cloves garlic	cooked broccoli)
2 shallots	pepper
fresh or dried herbs: oreg-	salt, to taste
ano, basil (fresh only),	2 tablespoons grated
marjoram	Parmesan

Skin, seed, and quarter the tomatoes.* Cut the zucchini
into cubes. Mince the garlic. In the food processor, or with a
sharp knife, cut up the shallots and herbs (if fresh).

Heat the oil in a nonstick pan, and lightly sauté the herbs
and fresh vegetables. Add the cooked peas or broccoli, cover
the pan, and steam this mixture for a minute, but no longer.

When the pasta is cooked, drain it and put it in a preheated bowl. Mix in the hot vegetables and season with pepper and salt, to taste. Top off with fresh-grated Parmesan.

---

*Tomatoes can be easily peeled if they are submerged for 10 seconds in boiling
water. The skin then comes off in big strips.

SPIRALS WITH FRESH ASPARAGUS
(Serves 4)

Spirals combine well with inch-long pieces of fresh, steamed asparagus. Shallots, minced ham, and grated cheese complete this felicitous match.

1 pound pasta (spirals, preferably)	2 shallots
1 pound fresh asparagus	3 tablespoons corn oil
¼ pound lean, sliced ham	pepper
	¼ cup grated Parmesan

Before boiling the pasta, prepare the sauce.

Steam the asparagus until it is nearly tender. Cut the stalks into inch-long pieces.

In food processor, mince the ham and shallots.

Heat the oil in a nonstick pan and sauté the ham and shallots briefly. When they are warmed up, add the asparagus and pepper.

Combine the sauce with hot, drained pasta. Sprinkle Parmesan over all.

Mushrooms are a good substitute for asparagus in this recipe, and considering the brevity of the asparagus season, are more likely to be used here. Slice and sauté ½ to 1 pound of them in the oil, along with the ham and shallots. Season sauce with marjoram, fresh or dried.

SPAGHETTINI WITH CLAMS
(Serves 4)

Buy 18 large quahogs (chowder clams) that are tightly closed. Wash them well in several pans of cold water. Place ½ cup water in the bottom of a large pot and bring to a boil. Add the clams and cover pot tightly. In 5 minutes or so, clams will open. As soon as they do, take the pot off the stove, remove the clam meat from the shells, and chop it in the food processor quite coarsely. Save the broth in the pot.

Boil the water for 1 pound of spaghettini while you make the sauce.

2 cups minced clam meat	chopped parsley
2 tablespoons corn oil	½ cup clam juice (from the
1 shallot (or 1 clove garlic)	pot)
pepper	½ cup dry white wine

Chop shallot with a very sharp knife or mince garlic in press. Cook this briefly in oil in nonstick pan. Add clams, pepper, and parsley, and sauté these lightly.

When pasta is almost cooked, add the clam juice and wine to the clam mixture and heat the sauce well. Combine with piping hot, drained spaghettini.

MACARONI SHELLS WITH MUSSELS
(Serves 4)

Wash mussels thoroughly in cold water, changing the water until it comes clear; this might mean 6 or 8 separate immersions. If you have time, soak them in cold water for an hour or so before steaming them. Should any barnacles cling to the shells, ignore them. They are tasteless, and usually fall off during the cooking process without injuring the flavor of the broth.

Steam the mussels in ½ cup dry vermouth or white wine until they open (5 minutes or so). Take the meat out of the shells, but don't chop it. Strain the cooking liquid, and set a cupful aside.

2 cups mussels	fresh thyme leaves (or 1
2 cloves garlic	tablespoon dried thyme)
2 shallots	1 cup cooking liquid
2 tablespoons corn oil	
generous amount chopped	
fresh parsley	

In food processor, chop garlic, shallots, and other herbs. Sauté them together briefly in hot oil in a nonstick pan. Add mussels and 1 cup of their cooking liquid, and heat until mixture is bubbling.

Combine, instantly, with hot, drained pasta.

SESAME NOODLES
(*Serves 6*)

Served at room temperature, these noodles are fiery hot in flavor. They improve in the refrigerator, and are especially useful over a busy weekend, when you need something delicious that doesn't require any work.

Unlike other recipes for pasta, this one asks you to cook the noodles first and then make the sauce.

1 8-ounce package Asian noodles*	2 tablespoons sesame paste
1 tablespoon sesame oil	2 tablespoons Tamari sauce
1 tablespoon corn oil	2 tablespoons water (or tea)
1½ teaspoons chili oil	½ teaspoon sugar
2 garlic cloves, minced	1 tablespoon sherry
½-inch piece gingerroot, peeled	2 chopped scallions

In a big pot of boiling water, cook noodles for 3 minutes, separating the strands with a fork. Drain and rinse in cold water. Place in bowl, and mix in the three oils.

For the sauce, put all the rest of the ingredients except the scallions into the food processor or blender, and mix them thoroughly. Pour this sauce over the noodles, add the chopped scallions, and chill in the refrigerator. Bring noodles back to room temperature before serving.

*Asian noodles, made without eggs, are sometimes known as "Japanese-style" noodles.

ZITI WITH SPINACH
(*Serves 4*)

This Sicilian dish is a simplified version of the cannelloni one gets in northern Italy. Essentially, it's cannelloni turned inside out, but it's a lot less rich.

1 box ziti (tubular maca-
    roni)
2 boxes frozen spinach,
    thawed and drained°
1 clove garlic, minced
1 tablespoon lemon juice
fresh-ground pepper
fresh-ground nutmeg

salt, to taste
3 tablespoons corn oil
½ cup ricotta (or cottage
    cheese, or combination of
    the two)
2 tablespoons grated
    Parmesan

While the pasta is cooking (it will take 12 minutes or so), whirl the spinach in the food processor. Drain the excess liquid from it. Mix into it the minced garlic and seasonings.

When pasta is nearly ready, heat the oil in a nonstick pan and sauté the spinach mixture in it until it's hot. Remove from the stove, add the cheeses, and combine immediately with the hot, drained pasta.

°Of course use fresh spinach, if you prefer. Wash 1½ pounds, steam it briefly until its volume is reduced, then continue with it as directed above.

Rice

Rice can be eaten hot or cold, alone or in combination with other foods. Brown rice is superior, in both taste and nutrition, but occasionally white rice (the converted kind, in which the nutrients have been retained) has its uses. Uncle Ben's rice, in both categories, is wonderfully reliable. However, other, less costly, kinds of brown rice can do as well. Don't follow the directions for cooking on the box.

To cook rice for 4 people, use ¾ cup rice to 1½ cups chicken stock. (I usually double this amount so I have plenty left over to use in the next few days.) Put rice and stock into a small, nonstick saucepan, cover, and when you hear it boil, then turn the heat down to low. White rice needs 17 minutes cooking time; cook brown rice for 30 minutes. Then remove pot from stove and let rice rest, covered, for 15 minutes. It will continue cooking on its own, during this time, and then will retain its heat for a suprisingly long while.

Instant rice is not to be thought of: not only is it tasteless, but it's filled with chemicals to speed up the cooking process. Nor is there any reason to buy rice with curry sauce or other added seasonings. It's easy to make your own interesting and spicy rice dishes (see recipes on the following pages).

If you are fortunate enough to get some wild rice, stretch it by combining it half-and-half with brown rice and cook it in chicken stock for 45 minutes.

Rice combines well with mussels (see page 181), especially when the rice is cooked in the mussel broth. Mushrooms are good with rice, too: raw if the rice is cold and cooked if the rice is hot.

Cold rice salad is a superb dish. Add colorful raw or lightly steamed vegetables — tomatoes, peppers, peas, or green beans, shallots and scallions. Water chestnuts, black olives, and capers make good accents, for texture as well as taste. Season rice salad with oil, vinegar, and a touch of Tamari sauce. It's also good laced with a sauce of mayonnaise and yogurt.

If rice without butter seems dry to you, try trickling a little dry vermouth over it. Or dribble a few drops of French wine vinegar on top and mix it in with a minced garlic clove.

BROWN RICE WITH APRICOT PURÉE
(*Serves 8*)

This handsome combination could serve as the middle (main) course of a rather unusual and elegant dinner. You might start with cold filets of sole in aspic (page 171). Then the rice dish could be followed by either cold asparagus or salad. For dessert, ricotta cheese and yogurt, topped with black currant jam and crème de cassis (page 200).

Rice

2 cups brown rice	4 cups chicken stock
½-inch piece gingerroot, grated	2 scallions

Put rice, ginger, and chicken stock in a saucepan, covered, and bring to a boil, then reduce the heat to low. Cook the rice for 30 minutes, then let it rest for 15 minutes off the stove.

Chop scallions into ½-inch slices and set aside.

Apricot Purée

½ pound dried California apricots	1 tablespoon honey
2 slices fresh gingerroot	½ teaspoon almond extract
1½ tablespoons dry mustard	2 tablespoons sherry
	watercress for garnish

Place apricots in just enough cold water to cover them and bring slowly to a simmer. Cook, covered, for 20 minutes or so until they are soft. Purée them, together with the gingerroot, in the food processor. Add seasonings and blend until smooth.

Mound the rice at one end of a large platter, and cover the top with chopped scallions. Heap up the apricots at the other end of the platter, with a mass of watercress in between.

EASTERN RICE DISH
(Serves 4)

This is a fine main dish. A big bowl of fresh skim-milk yogurt should be passed around with the rice, together with warm pita bread. Spinach salad with oranges (page 148) could follow.

If you have two cups of leftover rice, this is an excellent way to make use of it. If you are starting from scratch, you might want to make a pilaf, instead of boiling the rice.

If so, proceed as follows: using 1 tablespoon of oil (subtracted from the amount used in the sauce), sauté 1 cup of raw white converted rice in an enamel-lined pot. When rice is coated with oil, add 2 cups of hot chicken stock and simmer, covered, for 20 minutes.

Prepare a sauce:

½ cup chicken stock
1 tablespoon currants
2 tablespoons raisins
mixture of spices: a generous pinch of cumin, coriander, cardamom, nutmeg, and Szechuan pepper

2 small onions
2 cloves garlic
1-2 tablespoons pine nuts
2-3 tablespoons corn oil
1 teaspoon Tamari sauce
chopped parsley

Heat the chicken stock and put currants, raisins, and spices into it to soak, while you complete the dish.

In food processor, chop onions and garlic, and sauté them with pine nuts in the oil. Combine these with the chicken stock, season with Tamari sauce, and mix well. Stir into hot rice and top with chopped parsley.

Vegetables

Fresh vegetables are at their prime when they've just been picked by an alert farmer. There is a summertime bonanza, when local gardens and markets are showing forth a continuous progression. But in winter, things are almost as good. In New York we are getting astonishing vegetables all winter in the small markets operated by energetic Korean families. These heroes rise at two in the morning in order to be at the city's wholesale markets at four. Asian wisdom is bringing us more than freshness; it is offering us difference. Now we have snow peas, bok choy, fresh gingerroot, and Chinese parsley as part of our daily diet.

A steamer is now my choice for cooking all vegetables — the only exceptions being beets and artichokes. All other vegetables emerge, after brief cooking, moist, full of flavor and color, not to mention vitamins.

Steamers are for sale everywhere. In Asian shops, fragile-seeming bamboo steamers are sold, but the metal ones are more suitable for American kitchens. A layer of lettuce leaves makes a good foundation for vegetables, and removes them from direct contact with the metal. Although these steamers have two trays, I find I seldom use but one; on rare occasions, I steam potatoes in the bottom tray. Adding a few fresh herbs to the steaming water is a nice touch and easy to do if you have a summertime herb garden.

When you serve a variety of vegetables at a given meal, it's a good idea to vary the texture. One way of doing this is to purée one of them. The chefs of the nouvelle cuisine almost always do this as part of their emphasis on handsome presentation and diversity.

I use only two frozen vegetables, and these are backups, always kept in the freezer: peas and spinach. In the case of the first, I rely on them because the fresh pea season is so short. I generally serve them puréed (see page 137) and they are very successful. Except when I use fresh spinach in salad, I purée that vegetable, too.

ACORN SQUASH
(Serves 4)

Here is an interesting stuffing for acorn squash, which is an alternative to the more familiar one of well-seasoned minced spinach.

2 small acorn squash	2 mushrooms
1 slice bread for bread crumbs	1 onion
	½ cup skim-milk yogurt
1 large carrot, peeled and quartered	cayenne pepper

Cut the squash in halves and divest them of their seeds.

In blender, grind up 1 torn slice of bread to make bread crumbs.

In food processor or with a sharp knife, chop the vegetables coarsely. Mix them in a bowl with bread crumbs, yogurt, and pepper. Fill the squash with the vegetable mixture and place them in a baking dish. Add water to the bottom of the dish to keep moisture in the air. In preheated 350° oven, bake the squash for 40 minutes.

ARTICHOKES (FRENCH)

French artichokes grow beautifully in California and are harvested in early spring. At this season, they are abundant and cheap and they make an elegant first course.

Because artichokes are usually served in this country as a hot vegetable, with melted butter as sauce, it's a nice twist that a low-fat diet reverts to the original French mode, in which artichokes are served cold with a vinaigrette sauce. This means they need to be cooked ahead of time, and are therefore, ready for dinner when you are.

ARTICHOKES VINAIGRETTE
(Serves 4)

4 artichokes	lemon juice
1 garlic clove, minced	black pepper

Buy medium-sized artichokes. Cut off their bottom stalks and the top inch of their leaves. Rub the cut surfaces with lemon.

Fit the artichokes into a saucepan, together with some lemon juice, a minced garlic clove, and black pepper. Pour over them boiling water to the depth of an inch. Cover the pot and simmer artichokes for about 45 minutes. Test their bases with a fork to decide if they are done. Drain and cool before chilling in the refrigerator.

Prepare individual cups for the sauce, which is made of 2 tablespoons each of olive oil and red wine vinegar, and a chopped shallot. Add pepper, to taste.

ARTICHOKES (JERUSALEM)

This is an odd vegetable, which grows like a weed in a garden; the edible tubers are topped by six-foot sunflowers. But for some reason, when sold commercially (and called "sunchokes") Jerusalem artichokes become rare and expensive. In any case, steamed for 10 minutes or so and puréed until smooth, they are delicious, having the consistency of potatoes. Briefly steamed and sliced they are a crunchy addition to spinach salad.

ASPARAGUS

April is asparagus month in New York, when it's brought in from warm climates. June is asparagus time in New England home gardens and it's an entirely different vegetable, unavailable except to the industrious few. But never mind: the early import is wonderful.

Cut off the bottom of the stalks, wash and scrape the scales from the sides of a bunch of medium-thick fresh asparagus. Place the asparagus over boiling water in a steamer. They need about 12 minutes to cook, and then when they are on a platter, give them a good lashing of fresh lemon juice.

BEETS

I find that I'm very attracted to beets, especially to those with huge green leaves attached to their stalks. I like to use these, finely minced, in buttermilk soup (see page 68).

Then I like to eat the beets themselves, either hot (see below), or cold, as an hors d'oeuvre, when they are served, whole or quartered, on toothpicks. Another use is as a first course (see next page).

A third way to use beets is found in the beautiful, pink beet soup (described on page 66), in which the cooking water is primarily involved.

HOT BEETS

Cut off all but an inch of the red stems. Wash the beets thoroughly in cold, running water, being sure to get rid of every trace of dirt. Cover them with fresh, cold water and bring it to a boil. Simmer the beets, covered, for about 1 hour and let them cool in their cooking water. (Save this water for soup.)

When cool, the skins of the beets slip off easily, and they are ready to eat. If you are going to serve them immediately, they will still be warm enough. Sprinkle them lightly with fresh lemon juice, if you like. But if they are perfectly fresh, they will be exactly right as is.

COLD BEETS WITH BASIL
(Serves 6)

This makes a splendid-looking and -tasting first course, which could lead into a dinner of fish or chicken, accompanied by rice or bulgur. Later, a light salad of watercress and Boston lettuce would be a pleasing follow-up.

4–5 cooked beets	1 tablespoon lemon juice
½ cup fresh basil leaves	1 cup cottage cheese and
2 scallions, white and green	yogurt sauce (page 53)
parts	

Slice the beets and scallions with a sharp knife, and chop the basil in the food processor.

Mix basil and beets together in the sauce, with added lemon juice. Fill individual cups with beets and top off with sliced scallions.

If you like, you can reverse this: mix the scallions with the beets and use the basil for topping. Either way, this is a very good dish. Serve chilled.

BEET TOPS

Cook these as you would spinach (see page 139). Also, beet greens are excellent in buttermilk soup (page 68).

BROCCOLI
(1 bunch serves 3)

Broccoli is a year-round vegetable, good served hot in winter and cold in summer. Choose very dark green broccoli. Cut off the leaves and the bottom of the stalks. With a sharp knife, gently peel the outsides of the stalks. In a large steamer, cook the broccoli for 5 or 10 minutes, depending on its freshness. Serve whole or cut off the stalks and use only the floweret tops. (If you do this, purée the stalks in the food processor and blend them into hot consommé on another occasion.)

Hot broccoli is delicious seasoned with lemon juice, pepper, and a light sprinkling of fresh-grated Parmesan.

HOT BROCCOLI
WITH WALNUT SAUCE
(Serves 3)

Walnut sauce is slightly more elaborate than the one above.

1 bunch steamed broccoli	1-2 tablespoons lemon juice
1 tablespoon walnut oil	2 tablespoons chopped wal-
2 shallots	nuts.
1 clove garlic	

In food processor, chop walnuts and empty container. Then mince garlic and shallots together. In oil, in nonstick pan, sauté garlic and shallots. Mix with lemon juice and chopped walnuts, and pour this sauce over hot broccoli.

COLD BROCCOLI
WITH CAPER SAUCE
(Serves 6)

Freshly picked broccoli, steamed and chilled, can make a handsome centerpiece for a small supper party. Use two bunches of dark green broccoli, and make the following cold sauce by simply combining all ingredients:

1 cup yogurt mayonnaise	1-2 teaspoons Dijon
(page 55)	mustard
1 teaspoon lemon juice	2 tablespoons capers

Put the sauce into a small bowl, to serve separately.

Arrange the broccoli in the middle of a large platter. Have a mound of Great Northern beans (page 85) at one end of the platter and a group of hot baked stuffed tomatoes (page 140) at the other. With a loaf of fresh-baked bread, you have a small feast. For dessert: sliced oranges with candied orange peel (page 194).

BRUSSELS SPROUTS
(*Serves 4*)

These delicate, tiny cabbages used to be found only in supermarket packages, with large-sized sprouts buried under a top layer of small ones. It's best to select your own, one by one, in a vegetable market. Choose the smallest, and those of the darkest shade of green; 16 or 20 sprouts are plenty for 4 people.

Clean Brussels sprouts in cold water, and when you cut off the bottom stem, make a tiny X incision in the base. This will speed up the cooking process.

Steam them for 5 minutes, more or less, over bubbling chicken stock. Serve immediately, pouring over them a tablespoon or two of the stock and a sprinkling of caraway seeds.

CABBAGE

Cabbage is full of vitamin C, and it's cheap and available year-round. It's not a very chic dish at a dinner party. However, when you are hunkered down at home sometime with a few intimates, astonish them with one or the other of these two delicious offerings. Get a small head of fresh cabbage, and pull off the outer leaves. Cut out the hard core with a sharp knife, and quarter the rest of the leaves. Slice these thinly in the food processor.

HOT CABBAGE
(Serves 6)

Try this dish with bulgur pilaf (page 92) and some baked stuffed tomatoes (page 140) for a tasty vegetarian meal.

3 cups shredded cabbage
1 teaspoon corn oil
few drops sesame oil

1 tablespoon Tamari sauce
2 tablespoons chopped
   walnuts

Heat the oil in a large nonstick saucepan. Add the cabbage and Tamari sauce, and stir until cabbage is hot, which should take a couple of minutes.

Sprinkle with chopped walnuts, stir, and serve immediately.

COLE SLAW
(Serves 4)

Prepare a small head of cabbage as described above. If it isn't quite crisp, chill it in ice water for 10 minutes. Drain, and serve it with a sweet-sour dressing.

3 cups shredded cabbage
1 cup skim-milk yogurt
1 tablespoon sugar

1 tablespoon red wine
   vinegar
black pepper

Mix sauce in a salad bowl, add cabbage, and toss lightly.

CARROTS

Always buy carrots with their green tops intact, thus assuring yourself of their freshness and flavor.

Incidentally, carrots more than any other vegetable serve to show off the versatility of the food processor. They may be grated, sliced in rounds, or puréed.

GRATED CARROTS
(Serves 4 to 6)

A small mound of grated carrots is a colorful addition to any dinner plate. It's also a nice touch of crunchiness. Scrape the skins off 4 carrots and submit them to the grater of the food processor. Empty these into a serving bowl. They are good plain, but can be improved by a few drops of walnut oil, some lemon juice, and perhaps a sprinkling of pepper and nutmeg. Toss them lightly.

HOT CARROTS
(Serves 4)

With a vegetable peeler, scrape the skin off a pound of carrots. If you like, slice them in rounds in the food processor, or cut them with a knife in long strips. Steam them over boiling water for 6–10 minutes or so. They should be firm, but soft enough to be enjoyable.

Here is a nice sauce for them:

½ cup fresh orange juice (frozen is equally good: use ¼ cup undiluted) fresh-grated orange or lemon peel

⅛ teaspoon fresh-grated nutmeg
⅛ teaspoon powdered cloves

Mix all ingredients together in a saucepan, heat briefly, and pour over hot carrots.

CARROT AND ONION PURÉE
(Serves 6)

A superb purée is made of carrots and onions; the texture is luscious, the color a nice complement to servings of pale chicken and fish. By adding a few sprigs of watercress, you make a picture.

Because the process of puréeing reduces the volume of food, it's necessary to start with more carrots than usual.

2 bunches fresh carrots
2 onions
pepper and cardamom

Peel and cut into sections the onions and carrots. Steam them over boiling water for 10 minutes or until they are very soft. Whirl them in the food processor. Season with spices and serve very hot.

CAULIFLOWER
(1 head serves 4 to 6)

For a sort of orphan vegetable, cauliflower has become amazingly expensive in recent years. I find that I only really like it in the fall, when it is freshly harvested and can be eaten raw with a dip as an appetizer. However, I imagine this is only a temporary lapse in my affections, for in truth we need all the variety we can get in life. Purple cauliflower is a new development. In this diet, deprived of the heartening red color of meat, we should welcome such exciting departures as purple cauliflower.

Pull off the rough outside leaves of a perfect head of cauliflower — either pure white or purple — and wash it in cold water. Pull apart the flowerets, and cut off the bottom of the stalks.

Steam the flowerets for 5 minutes or so, depending on the freshness. Serve with pepper and a sprinkling of fresh-grated Parmesan.

WHITE CAULIFLOWER
AND BROCCOLI

A cold salad can be effective-looking and -tasting when you combine these two. Arrange lightly steamed vegetables on a large platter and chill. Thin strips of raw red pepper can be used to enhance the appearance.

Sprinkle over these a sauce made of equal amounts of lemon juice and Tamari sauce, and some fresh-ground pepper.

BAKED PURPLE CAULIFLOWER
(Serves 4)

This is a fine dish for a late-autumn evening, when using the oven provides welcome warmth. In a 375–400° oven, you could cook all of the following: roast chicken for 1 hour (see page 153), baked sweet potatoes for the same amount of time, and, for the last 15 minutes of the hour, the dish of baked purple cauliflower described below. The colors should be pleasing: add a couple of sprigs of watercress to each plate to provide emphasis and crisp coolness.

Steam the flowerets of a head of purple cauliflower over boiling water for 5 minutes, more or less.

Place them in a shallow baking dish that has been lightly swept with oil. Top them up with a crumbly mixture:

1 cup fresh bread crumbs (see page 25)	1 tablespoon minced parsley
1 tablespoon safflower oil	1 tablespoon lemon juice
fresh-grated nutmeg	pepper

Sauté the bread crumbs in the oil until they are toasted. Add nutmeg, parsley, lemon juice, and pepper, and mix well. Sprinkle this mixture over the cauliflower, and bake the dish for 15 minutes in a moderately hot (375°) oven.

CELERY

A bunch of celery, topped by pale green leaves, is a thing of beauty and a paradigm of usefulness.

The outside stalks and especially the leaves flavor stocks

and soups. The middle stalks can be stuffed with a cottage cheese and yogurt mixture (see page 52), cut into inch-long sections, each topped with a bit of anchovy, and served for hors d'oeuvres. The inside stalks, slender and delicate, are ideal for eating raw, without any help from the outside.

POACHED CELERY
(Serves 4)

This is so good and so simple to make, I wonder why we don't have it every night. Use the middle stalks.

8 stalks of celery	1-2 tablespoons tarragon,
½ cup chicken stock	fresh or dried
½ cup white wine	pepper

Trim the stalks and slice them into thin strips. Place these flat in a shallow baking dish and cover them with the other ingredients. Cook, covered, in a moderate oven (350°) for 15 minutes.

CELERY ROOT

Celery root, also known as celeriac, is a large, brown, rough-skinned root vegetable. It appears in a virtually raw state in French restaurants, sliced in julienne strips, wrapped in a mustard sauce. Delectable as this is, it's no project for a home cook. The peeling alone is enough to put you off. But when the root has been steamed for ½ hour or so, until it is tender, then the skin comes off relatively easily.

CELERY ROOT AND POTATO PURÉE
(*Serves 6*)

This delicious purée is a fine hot vegetable dish.

4 medium potatoes	pepper
4 medium celery roots	salt, to taste

Steam the unpeeled vegetables together for ½ hour or so. Cool and then peel them. In food processor, purée them, and before serving — if necessary — reheat them and season with pepper and salt, to taste.

This dish like other puréed vegetable dishes, can be quickly converted into soup, should you think well of the idea. Heat up 1½ or 2 quarts of chicken stock. Put the purée into the blender, add some of the hot stock, and blend them together. Add this mixture to the rest of the hot chicken stock, and stir thoroughly. This will provide enough soup for 6 people.

CHESTNUTS

Chestnuts are the only nut totally lacking in fat. This seems odd because they taste so rich. In the United States, we think of them as a vegetable. But the French use them in desserts, coated with sugar. Hot roasted chestnuts are sold in winter on the streets of large cities, and they give off a delicious smell and a lovely taste. Chestnut stuffing for turkey — heavenly — is described on page 162.

Another nice way to use chestnuts is to bake them, and serve them piping hot in their shells, accompanied by a glass of red wine or port. This is particularly welcome on a leisurely late afternoon or after dinner in the dark of winter. Prepare the chestnuts by slashing the side of each one with a sharp knife, and bake them in a 400° oven for 1 hour.

PURÉED CHESTNUTS
(Serves 4)

We would eat chestnuts a lot oftener if they were easier to peel. After slashing the side of each chestnut, steam them for 20 minutes or so, and then peel off the outer shell as well as the inner skin. It doesn't matter if they crumble since you're going to purée them anyway.

1 pound chestnuts	salt, to taste
2 stalks celery	chopped parsley, for garnish
pepper	

Steam the chestnuts together with the celery for 20 minutes or so, before shelling and skinning them. Purée them with the celery in the food processor, season with pepper and salt, to taste, and serve topped with a little chopped parsley.

CORN

A traditional American favorite, fresh corn is best eaten the same day it's been picked. Look for it in late July, August, and early September at roadside stands. (Corn in supermarkets, year round, is inevitably too old to be worth cooking.)

The association of corn with butter need trouble you not at all. Once you've tasted fresh corn without butter, I think you'll agree that it's superior. No butter running down over your chin, either.

STEAMED CORN ON THE COB

Shuck the newly picked ears of corn just before eating them. Children and houseguests can be dragooned into doing this.

Since the sheer bulk of corn on the cob prevents us from using the steamer, I use the big pot that we cook pasta and lobster in. Cover the bottom of such a pot to the depth of 1 inch with a combination of water and skim milk. Bring this to a boil, quickly pop in the corn, and cover pot. The corn will be juicy and ready to eat in 5 minutes.

GRILLED CORN ON THE COB

There's nothing fast about this method of grilling corn, but if you're on a beach picnic on a beautiful evening, it's nice to have things to do, to draw the time out longer. Fill a pail with seawater. Pull down the husks of a dozen ears of corn and soak them in the water for ½ hour. Then draw the husks back up over the corn and tie the top of each ear tight, using one of the outside leaves. The ears of corn may now be roasted on the campfire, and with an occasional turning, they should be delectable in about 15 minutes.

CUCUMBERS

Cucumbers are a versatile vegetable. They combine well with other foods, and stand alone with distinction. With a special thin-slicer, an accessory to a food processor that needs to be bought separately, cucumbers can be cut paper-thin in two seconds. These slices are especially good for cucumber sandwiches, made with thin-sliced bread.

Thick slices of cucumber are best for hors d'oeuvres, served on top of quartered slices of bread, lightly stroked with yogurt mayonnaise (page 55). Scatter chopped herbs — fresh dill, mint, chives, and/or parsley — on top.

Most of the year, cucumbers appear in shops with their skin waxed for travel. They need to be skinned, seeded, rinsed, and dried. I use them as a last resort.

Other, better cucumbers are:

Native cucumbers. In season, these are best of all. You can scrape off some of the peel, run a fork down the outside, and slice them. They may then be spread out to drain, and after 15 minutes, dried off. They will be crisp and tasty, their edges prettily serrated.

English cucumbers. These are now grown in California and sent to market sheathed in plastic. Both skin and seeds are edible.

Kerby cucumbers. Unwaxed and therefore perishable, these are used mostly for pickling. Some gourmet cooks prefer them; I find them somewhat pallid.

CUCUMBERS IN YOGURT
(*Serves 6*)

Serve these cucumbers as a side dish with chicken curry (see page 159).

3 small cucumbers (or 1 English cucumber)	2 scallions
1 garlic clove	1–2 cups skim-milk yogurt
	chopped mint leaves

Slice the cucumbers thinly, and spread them out on a platter for 15 minutes. Pat them dry.

With a sharp knife chop the scallions. Mince the garlic.

Mix scallions, garlic, and cucumbers together in a bowl with the yogurt, and top off with chopped fresh mint leaves.

HOT CUCUMBERS AND GREEN PEPPER
(*Serves 2*)

This is a lovely hot dish, which with some cornmeal (page 93) could give you supper on an off night.

1 English cucumber (or 2 or 3 small ones)	1 teaspoon dried thyme
½ green pepper	pepper
1 onion	salt, to taste
1 teaspoon safflower oil	½ cup yogurt

In food processor, thinly slice onion and pepper. Empty container. Then, using the thick slicer, prepare cucumber.

In a nonstick saucepan, heat oil, sauté onion and pepper, then add the cucumber and thyme. Simmer, covered, for 15 minutes. Taste for seasoning, and add pepper and salt, to taste.

Remove pan from stove and gently stir in yogurt. Serve immediately.

BROILED EGGPLANT IN TOMATO SAUCE
(Serves 4)

This dish, hearty and delicious, is derived from the justly famous (if very rich) eggplant parmigiana, an invention of Italian-American restaurateurs. In their kitchens, the slices of eggplant are deep-fried in boiling oil. The result can occasionally be soggy; it's always fattening. Here the eggplant slices are broiled with no oil at all. This makes a terrific dinner, with a big green salad and Italian bread. For dessert, yogurt with grapes and apricots (page 200).

1 large eggplant	½ cup grated Parmesan
2 cups tomato sauce (see	cheese
page 57)	½ cup minced parsley
¼ pound mozzarella cheese	

Remove the stem from the eggplant, and scrub it only if it is heavily waxed. Slice it into ½-inch-thick portions. Preheat the broiler to 500°, and cover the broiling pan with aluminum foil. Arrange the eggplant slices thereon and broil them for 5 minutes on each side, or until they are lightly browned and crisp.

In the food processor, chop the mozzarella first, then the parsley separately, and finally the Parmesan. Prepare the tomato sauce (see page 57). You've now done all the hard work, and can leave the various ingredients, covered, on the kitchen counter until it's time for the final assembly.

Twenty-five minutes before dinner, preheat the oven to 350°. Into a shallow baking dish, pour a thin coating of tomato sauce. On this, place two layers of eggplant, each topped with chopped mozzarella. Pour the rest of the tomato sauce over all, and sprinkle on the minced parsley and Parmesan.

Bake this dish for 15 minutes, and then, for a final browning, turn up the heat to 500° in the broiler and slip the baking dish under this heat for a couple of minutes until the top is crisp and bubbly.

GREEN BEANS

In summer, small, freshly picked green beans are a delicacy unparalleled. All you need to do is wash them, pick off their stem ends, and steam them for 5 minutes. If you like, add to them some fresh tarragon leaves that have been softened in white wine vinegar.

PURÉE OF GREEN BEANS
(*Serves 4*)

When beans are not absolutely fresh and young, more help is needed. One good idea is to purée them.

1½ pounds green beans*	1 teaspoon lemon juice
1 small onion	1 teaspoon cumin (optional)
1 teaspoon parsley	

Steam the beans and onion for 8 minutes or so. In the food processor, grind them coarsely, and add parsley and lemon juice. If the beans seem to lack moisture, add a little yogurt or hot chicken stock. If they taste flat, add a teaspoon of freshly crushed cumin seeds.

*Since puréeing has a way of reducing the volume, it's necessary to use more vegetables than usual.

GREEN BEAN SALAD
(Serves 4)

This is an excellent way to serve green beans.

1½ pounds cooked green beans	1 tablespoon walnut oil
1-2 tablespoons chopped walnuts	1 teaspoon red wine vinegar
½ red onion	½ teaspoon Dijon mustard
	cayenne pepper

With a sharp knife, chop the walnuts.

In the food processor, thinly slice the onion.

Make the vinaigrette dressing of oil, vinegar, mustard, and pepper.

Put the beans in a bowl, scatter onion and walnuts over them, and pour on the dressing. Serve cold or at room temperature.

MUSHROOMS

Fresh mushrooms are best bought from open containers — either oval baskets or square boxes — so you can select the best ones by hand. Choose white-topped mushrooms that have their tops so closely curled about their stems that the brown underside is invisible.

Mushrooms are wonderful raw, either for hors d'oeuvres or in salad. Cooked, they combine well with rice and other grains, with spinach and green beans.

To cook them you need only slice them and heat them briefly in a nonstick pan. If you are going to stuff raw mushroom caps for hors d'oeuvres (see page 46), then make duxelles from the stalks (see below).

DUXELLES

Duxelles is a dry mixture of finely minced mushrooms and shallots that can be stored in the refrigerator for as much as a week, and used as a flavoring for marinades, soups, and sauces. Since it can be made successfully from mushroom stalks that might otherwise be thrown away, it is an economical venture.

stalks from 1 pound fresh   1 teaspoon corn oil
   mushrooms   1 tablespoon Madeira
4 shallots

In food processor, whirl the mushroom stalks briefly, and squeeze them dry in a clean dish towel. (This hastens the cooking process.)

Without washing the food processor, mince the shallots.

Heat oil in a nonstick pan and cook the mushrooms and shallots together, turning them until the moisture is absorbed. Add Madeira, and again stir until it is integrated. The mixture in the pan is dry when it is fully cooked.

Spoon the duxelles into a jar, cover tightly, and refrigerate until you want to use it.

POACHED WHITE ONIONS
(Serves 8)

Small white onions are a delicacy, poached in a wine sauce with herbs. They are a traditional offering at a holiday feast, along with the roast turkey.

Before cooking, they need to be stripped of their skin, which comes off with more difficulty than does that of yellow onions. But if you drop them into a pot of boiling water for 10 seconds, drain them, and nip off their two ends, their skins will slip right off.

24 small white onions,   1 bay leaf, minced
   peeled   1 tablespoon dried thyme
½ cup chicken stock   minced fresh parsley
½ cup white wine

In a shallow baking dish place the peeled onions, liquids, minced bay leaf, and thyme. Cover the dish with aluminum foil and bake for 30 minutes in a 350° oven. Uncover the dish for a final 15 minutes. Sprinkle parsley over top.

Traditionally, onions are simmered on top of the stove, with the cook giving the pot an occasional shake so as to redistribute the onions. By baking them in a shallow pan, you give all the onions equal heat.

GREEN PEAS

Fresh green peas make a brief appearance in spring. These should be shelled just before eating, steamed for 5 minutes, and anointed with pepper and salt, to taste. You'll never miss the butter.

PURÉED PEAS
(Serves 8)

One of the prettiest and most delectable of the vegetable dishes in this book, puréed peas here are made from frozen peas. When steamed, they retain their brilliant green color.

3 boxes frozen peas, thawed
2 cucumbers
2 shallots
½ teaspoon sugar

fresh-ground pepper
1 tablespoon ricotta (optional)

Peel cucumbers and cut them into big pieces. Steam them for 15 minutes, until they are quite soft.

Add peas and shallots to the steamer, and continue cooking for 5 minutes more, when all vegetables should be tender and the peas will still hold their color.

Empty the vegetables into the food processor, add pepper and sugar, and whirl them until you have a smooth purée. If you like, add ricotta. Put this into the top of a double boiler so it may be reheated before it's served.

SNOW PEAS

Fresh and relatively cheap in Asian markets, snow peas are a luxury item in gourmet grocery shops. In recent years they have often been grown in home gardens. They are both ornamental and tasty, providing wonderful crunch. They are excellent served raw for hors d'oeuvres. They are good in all salads and in cold rice. Briefly steamed, they make a fine green vegetable, unadorned.

POTATOES

Potatoes are survival food, but they also can be an exquisite eating experience. And this, mind you, without frying them in deep fat or slathering them with butter after they have been boiled or baked.

A baked potato is a meal in itself. On a night when you are by yourself and too tired to cook, do just one thing before collapsing on the couch with a drink or snoozing in the tub. Put an Idaho (or a sweet) potato into the toaster (or regular) oven and turn it up high, to 450°. Set the timer for an hour (or less depending on the potato's size). When it's ready to eat, its skin will be crisp, its insides meltingly soft. Have a bowl of fresh skim-milk yogurt to go with it. By this time you may have the energy to find a few radishes, scallions, or sprigs of watercress in the refrigerator. Soon you will have effortlessly prepared a quite perfect meal.

STEAMED NEW POTATOES

The least starchy of potatoes are small new ones, preferably beige-colored. Wash them and steam them for 20 minutes. They will be full of moisture and you won't want to add anything to them except perhaps a generous sprinkling of finely minced parsley and/or dill. These potatoes are elegant companions for chicken or fish.

SPINACH

The classic health food, spinach is admired also for its taste, its elegant dark green color, and its adaptability. It makes a fine foil for pale foods such as pasta, chicken, and fish. A few fresh leaves of spinach lend vividness to sallow salads; other salads are made with spinach alone.

Frozen spinach, however, is amazingly good, and for cooked dishes it's a big time saver. I get the whole-leaf version, which seems to taste better than the chopped variety. After thawing, it needs to be minced in the food processor, heated up, and — before being used — drained of any excess water.

SPINACH WITH PINE NUTS
(Serves 4)

This is a glamorous way to serve spinach.

2 boxes frozen spinach, thawed (or 2 pounds fresh spinach)
1 teaspoon corn oil
1 tablespoon pine nuts
1 clove garlic, minced
1 tablespoon Madeira
pepper
fresh-grated nutmeg

If using frozen spinach, whirl it in the food processor, and then drain it of excess water.

If using fresh spinach, wash it, and steam it (without additional water) in a big covered pot for 2 or 3 minutes, until it is wilted. Mince it in the food processor, and drain thoroughly.

Heat up 1 teaspoon oil in large pan, and toast the pine nuts lightly in it. Add garlic, minced spinach, and Madeira; cook, covered, for a few minutes until spinach is heated. Season with pepper, nutmeg, and salt to taste, and serve hot.

TOMATOES

In principle, tomatoes are available year-round, but as everyone knows, tomatoes — like green peas — are best eaten right out of the garden. If you live in the Northeast, and have a garden or farming neighbors, August and September are two months of abundance. We tend to eat tomatoes almost every day in season.

We have them sliced with chopped mozzarella and fresh basil leaves. We have gazpacho (page 71) and tomato sandwiches, made with crusty bread, into which thin-sliced red onion and homemade mayonnaise are introduced. Fresh sliced tomatoes, dribbled over with a little olive oil, look handsome arranged on a bed of young spinach leaves. Fresh tomato sauce (page 57) is wonderful on fish or rice. An unexpected (and therefore very welcome) dish at this time of year is baked tomatoes (below) or broiled tomatoes, stuffed with pesto (page 141).

Recently it has seemed that the two best wintertime tomatoes are cherry tomatoes and Italian plum tomatoes. Both are good in salads, divested of their seeds and white pulp. They are both also good combined with fresh, chopped fennel.

But usually during the winter, when incorporating tomatoes in a cooked dish, I prefer canned Italian plum tomatoes to the fresh kind, and here they appear in tomato sauce (page 57) and in the two fish stews on pages 172 and 173.

BAKED STUFFED TOMATOES

As mentioned, baked tomatoes excite interest when you've spent weeks eating raw ones. Actually, they are a wonderfully useful dish year-round.

Slice the tomatoes in half and cut out all their seeds and any white pulp. Invert the cut tomatoes on a board and let them drain. Then arrange them on a shallow baking dish and stuff them with some of the following:

fresh bread crumbs (page 25)
pepper
minced garlic

finely chopped onion
fresh herbs: parsley, basil, or oregano

You might want to add:

a little leftover bulgur or rice
grated Parmesan

Bake stuffed tomatoes in a 375° oven for 15 minutes.

BROILED TOMATOES

Cut tomatoes in half, divest them of their seeds, and invert them on a board to drain. Fill them with pesto (page 58).

Preheat broiler to 500°, and cook the tomatoes for about 8 minutes.

Salad

When you bring salad greens in from the market, it's a good idea to wash them immediately, dry them in a salad spinner, and put them in plastic bags, enclosing a lot of air (see page 24). This keeps them dry and crisp for days.

It's interesting to have a mixture of greens in a salad. Ruby red lettuce, my favorite, tender in taste and texture, goes well with Belgian endive, Boston lettuce, romaine, watercress, escarole, or arugula. It's nice to add a few leaves of fresh sorrel or spinach, and in very early spring, violet leaves or dandelion greens.

It's also interesting to have a variety of vegetables in most salads. They then become treasure troves, yielding up mysteries as one delves into their depths. Mushrooms, radishes, fennel, red onions and scallions, bits of chopped ham and mozzarella lend contrast to the expected tomatoes and cucumbers. It's good to marinate the vegetables in a garlicky dressing, so that it's easy to combine them with the chilled greens just before serving.

If you are going to add tomatoes to salad, they should be seeded, and any pulp excised, before being used. Allow them to drain before putting them into the salad bowl. Cucumbers also should be seeded and drained for 15 minutes or so, for they are equally capable of making a salad soggy.

One salad made without greens is composed of oranges and red onions, sliced together in the food processor, with its own dressing built in. (For two people use 2 oranges and ½ red onion.)

Under the less-is-more rubric, make half the amount of salad dressing that you usually do and see if it isn't an improvement.* Too much salad dressing (with a residue in the bowl after the salad is finished) is much worse than too little.

* See page 28 of the Introduction.

ESCAROLE AND FENNEL SALAD
(*Serves 4*)

This salad is an Italian idea, easily adapted if you can find some really fresh fennel, topped by long, feathery stalks. Cut these off and use only the bulb.

1 small head of escarole	1 teaspoon lemon juice
1 fennel bulb	pepper
2 tablespoons olive oil	salt, to taste

Wash, dry, and chill the escarole. Just before serving, slice the fennel bulb into thin vertical or horizontal strips. Mix together the greens and the fennel slices, and add oil, lemon juice, pepper, and salt, to taste.

GREEK SALAD

This is a good salad for a party. You can prepare it ahead of time, using an enormous bowl, and keep it chilled in the refrigerator. Add the vinaigrette only at the very last moment.

romaine lettuce	black Greek olives, pitted
radishes	fresh oregano leaves
scallions	feta cheese
red onion	vinaigrette dressing (page
cucumbers	56)
tomatoes	

With a sharp knife, thinly slice the radishes and scallions. If you are including more than one red onion, use the food processor to thinly slice these. If the cucumbers are neither native nor of the English type, peel, seed, and drain them. Seed the tomatoes, and drain them, too.

It's fun to prepare the salad. Arrange lettuce (torn into small pieces) at the bottom of the bowl and carefully place the vegetables in circular layers. At the top, place the chopped scallions and black olives.

Scatter the oregano leaves and feta cheese (crumbled by hand) over the top just before the presentation. (There might be some cheers.) At the last, pour on the vinaigrette and toss.

PERSIMMON AND GRAPEFRUIT SALAD
(Serves 4)

Persimmons need to be perfectly ripe (otherwise they make your mouth pucker) but they are a wonderful midwinter treat. Persimmons and grapefruit make a splendid pair.

Belgian endive is another midwinter offering. Combined with watercress, it makes a superb salad. Put all these together and you have something quite special.

1 bunch watercress

2 heads Belgian endive

1-2 ripe persimmons

1 grapefruit, flesh and juice

1-2 tablespoons olive oil

Wash, dry, and chill watercress and endive, snapping the stalks off the first and carefully separating the leaves of the second. Just before serving, halve the grapefruit, cut out its sections, and squeeze 2 or 3 tablespoons of the juice over these. Add to this the cut-up persimmon and toss with the oil.

Arrange the greens in a salad bowl and put the fruits on top. This is a nice salad to show off before you toss it.

SPINACH SALAD WITH ORANGES
(*Serves 4*)

This is good in winter when oranges are abundant, but perhaps it's even better in summer when they become a bit unusual. In summer, also, fresh garden spinach is easy to find.

½ pound fresh spinach
1–2 California navel oranges

Wash spinach in cold water. Cut off the stalks and whirl the leaves dry, as you would with lettuce. Chill them in a plastic bag, enclosing air.

Peel and divide into sections the oranges. When you are ready to serve the salad, scatter the orange pieces over the cold spinach leaves.

Make a mustardy dressing:

1 shallot, minced
1 tablespoon red wine (or sherry wine) vinegar
3 tablespoons olive and corn oil

½ teaspoon lemon juice
1 tablespoon Dijon mustard

Pour over the prepared salad and serve at once.

Chicken and Turkey

Chicken is one of the four cornerstones of this modern method of cooking. The others are whole grains, vegetables, and yogurt.

The delicacy and succulence of chicken are matched by its adaptability; it goes well with practically everything. The smaller the chicken, the more tender the meat and the lower the fat content. Most of the fat in chicken is visible; it's in the skin and right under the skin in chunks. Both skin and fat can be pulled off and thrown away. In the case of broiled or roasted chickens, however, the skin is needed as protection for the flesh during cooking. When chicken comes to the table, a diner can choose to eat the skin or discard it.

POACHED CHICKEN

A 3½- to 4-pound chicken, cut up and simmered in wine, water, herbs, and vegetables for 20 minutes, becomes the fundamental ingredient for dozens of dishes. The stock, simmered with the discarded bones for an hour or two, makes a later appearance in sauces, soups, and as a cooking medium for rice and grains.

Buy a chicken whole (that's the cheapest way) and cut it up into quarters.* Strip off the large chunks of fat near the

---

* It's the cheapest way, but not the fastest. For occasions when you want to quickly make a dish using cooked chicken, I recommend using boned chicken breasts. They can be sliced in half and poached for 5 minutes in a small

tail, and wash the chicken pieces in cold water. Leave the skin on; it is easy to remove after cooking.

In a large pot, place 8 cups of water. Add:

2 onions, quartered	1 bay leaf
2 garlic cloves, unpeeled	1 tablespoon dried thyme
2 celery stalks, with leaves	(or twice as much if fresh)
2 carrots	black peppercorns, lightly
parsley stalks (or sprigs of	crushed
fresh parsley)	

Bring this mixture to a boil, then cover and simmer it for 10 minutes or so. Then add the chicken pieces plus:

1 cup white wine (or ½ cup light vermouth)
1-2 tablespoons rice wine vinegar

Simmer chicken, covered, for 20 minutes and remove from pot with tongs. When cool enough to handle, strip the skin off the meat and throw away. Pull the meat off the bones in large chunks and refrigerate in covered container.

Return bones to the pot and let stock simmer uncovered for another hour or two. This adds flavor and nutrition and allows the stock to reduce a bit. Cool stock, strain it into a bowl, and store it in refrigerator for at least 8 hours. By this time all the fat will have risen to the surface and formed a solid mass. It may then be easily lifted off and thrown away. This last step is, clearly, the crucial one for this cookbook. The stock will be light and delicious.

Poached chicken can be used in dozens of ways. It happily marries with cold rice, warm beans, and hot vegetables. It makes splendid curry (page 159). Variations on chicken salad appear on pages 155–156, and one of the best dishes in this book, chicken with dill and capers, is described on page 157–158, and advocated for a party.

---

amount of stock made of chicken broth and white wine. They are then ready to be put to immediate use in all the following dishes that demand 2 or more cupfuls of cooked chicken.

HOT ROAST CHICKEN
(Serves 4)

On a low-fat diet it's better to have two small roast chickens than one large one. Huge chickens (so-called roasters weighing 6 or 7 pounds) have sat around a lot and put on fat. Cook the chicken on a wire rack fitted into a roasting pan.

Wash and dry a 4-pound chicken. Rub lemon juice inside the cavity and over the skin. Roast it as is, or, if you like, slather the bird with a mixture of yogurt and Dijon mustard — a couple of tablespoons of each — into which you have introduced a healthy handful of fresh herbs, finely chopped. These herbs should be powerful: rosemary, oregano, or dill. Use some of them to stuff the chicken's cavity, along with an onion cut in half.

Preheat the oven to 400° and roast the chicken for about 70 minutes. After cooking, let it rest for 15 minutes before carving to allow the juices to settle inside. Cover it with a damp dish towel for this period.

In summer a cold roast chicken in the icebox is a very pleasant resource as immediate picnic food, stuffing for sandwiches, or an attractive offering at lunch or supper.

BROILED CHICKEN
(Serves 4)

We have broiled chicken often. Small birds, cut in quarters, cook in minutes, and their flesh is tender. We like it rather spicily seasoned, but sometimes I simply rub lemon juice and a fresh herb such as tarragon over the chicken pieces and let them marinate for an hour or so. They then broil in a very hot oven (500°) for 10 minutes on their flesh side. The skin side may be cooked at slightly lower heat (450°) for 15 minutes.

After dinner, save the bones to make stock. Add them to the bag of bones in the freezer (see page 64).

On those occasions when I prepare a marinade, I particularly like one that is French in seasoning, and another that is Chinese.

MUSTARD MARINADE
(For 1 chicken)

2 shallots

1 tablespoon minced fresh parsley

2 tablespoons Dijon mustard

3–4 tablespoons lemon juice

1 tablespoon dried thyme*

1 teaspoon dried tarragon*

In the food processor, chop the shallots and parsley. Combine them with the mustard, lemon juice, and dried herbs in a small bowl. With a spoon, spread this mixture onto the chicken (which has been split, cleaned, washed, and thoroughly dried). Marinate the chicken for ½ hour or more before broiling for approximately 10 minutes on each side.

* If you use fresh herbs, double the amounts, and chop them with the parsley and shallots.

GINGER MARINADE
(For 1 chicken)

1 onion

2 cloves garlic

2 slices gingerroot

2 tablespoons Tamari sauce

1 teaspoon lemon juice

In the food processor, chop the onion, garlic, and gingerroot. Add these vegetables to the Tamari and lemon juice and brush this mixture over the chicken. Let it rest for ½ hour or more before broiling.

CHICKEN WITH TREE EAR MUSHROOMS
(Serves 4)

It is odd for me, a person who thinks nothing of presoaking dried beans for 8 hours, to have to admit that I was daunted for years by dried mushrooms because of their need to be reconstituted in hot water. Now I have overcome my prejudice, and am delighted to find the preparation simple and the result indescribably delicious.

Tree ear and cloud mushrooms are one and the same, and are imported from China. Wash them and soak them in hot water while you prepare the chicken dish. When the mushrooms have soaked for 20 minutes, drain and dry them. Cut off any rough stem portions. Slice the remaining winglike parts or chop them in the food processor.

¼ cup dried tree ear, or cloud, mushrooms	2 cups poached chicken (page 151)
1 clove garlic	1 teaspoon Szechuan pepper
1-2 scallions	1 tablespoon sesame oil
2 tablespoons fresh Chinese parsley	1 tablespoon corn oil
	2 tablespoons Tamari sauce

Mince the garlic and cut up the scallions (both white and green parts). Shred the chicken, pulling it to pieces with your fingers in the Chinese manner. Crush the peppercorns. Prepare the presoaked mushrooms.

After this work, it only takes minutes to cook the dish. In hot oil, sauté garlic, scallions, and Szechuan pepper. Add the mushrooms and cook until they are crisp. Finally, add the chicken, Chinese parsley, and Tamari sauce and heat thoroughly.

This is marvelous served with brown rice, cooked with a bay leaf and some fresh or dried thyme, and tomatoes — baked, freshly sliced, or tossed in a salad.

CHICKEN SALAD

Equally good in winter or summer, chicken salad can be served mixed with a lot of finely torn-up lettuce leaves, on a bed of fresh spinach, or surrounded by watercress. Sliced tomatoes or cherry tomatoes can decorate it.

Basically, chicken salad is made from the chicken you have

poached (see page 151), plus some crisp vegetable such as celery or fennel, cut in tiny pieces. Besides this you might want to add some chopped red onion, walnuts, or some whole green grapes.

The chicken, cut into bite-sized pieces, can be marinated for an hour or so in oil and lemon juice. Drain this marinade, add the crisp vegetables, fruits, and/or nuts, and wrap all in a skim-milk yogurt–mayonnaise dressing (page 55). Season with a dash of mustard or curry powder. Cayenne pepper can be helpful, and Tamari sauce, as well.

Crisp-skinned baked potatoes go well here. So does a bowl of fresh-grated carrots, seasoned with a little nutmeg and lemon juice. A loaf of French bread, warmed in the oven, would complete this meal. For dessert: fresh fruit in season.

CHICKEN IN ASPIC
(*Serves 6*)

Chicken in aspic is beautiful for a summertime celebration. Nasturtium flowers and leaves make a particularly felicitous decoration, but other flowers and/or herbs could do as well. These are embedded, together with plump slices of white chicken, in a transparent aspic.

Poach the chicken the day before (page 151); the stock will then have time to chill so it can be defatted.

8 slices cooked chicken	¼ cup cold water
2 cups chicken stock	nasturtium flowers and
1 cup white wine	leaves for decoration
1 package gelatin	

The chicken stock, combined with the white wine, must be strengthened by reduction to 2 cups. But before doing this, you may want to clarify the stock in order to produce an exquisitely clear aspic. It's a rather entertaining process, as long as you do it only once a year. For clarfying stock, you need:

1 egg white
1 eggshell, crushed
Madeira wine

Use a saucepan to beat the egg white with a wire whisk. Add to it the crushed eggshell, then pour over this 2 cups of cold chicken stock. Cook over moderate heat until it comes to a boil, then reduce heat to low and simmer the stock for 15 minutes. Strain through a cheesecloth-lined strainer into another saucepan.

Add the white wine to the clear stock, and cook this brew quite rapidly until it is reduced to 2 cups. If you find you have overdone it, replenish with a little Madeira.

Measure out ¼ cup cold water, add gelatin, and stir. When this mixture is thick (3 or 4 minutes), add it to the hot stock and blend well. Pour a little of this liquid (perhaps ½ cup) into the bottom of a shallow serving dish and chill it for an hour, by which time the stock will have jelled.

Wash the nasturtium flowers and leaves under cold, running water and pluck off their stems. Arrange them, together with the chicken slices, on the chilled jellied stock. Pour on the remaining liquid and chill again until the aspic is quite firm. This might be a matter of a couple of hours, or perhaps more.

You might have soup first — zucchini soup (page 77) would be good either hot or cold. Fresh green beans would be a fine accompaniment for the aspic, together with warm French bread. For dessert: apricot fluff (page 00) would be an ideal conclusion to this light and elegant feast.

CHICKEN WITH DILL AND CAPERS
(Serves 8)

Served cold, this is a superb dish for a party. If you can manage to poach two chickens the day before (see page 151), you will have very little to do on the day of the party. The meal might also include steamed new potatoes (page 138) and a big bowl of hot puréed carrots (page 125).

This recipe was originally inspired by one of Michael Field's called Dilled Fish Salad. It provides a rather good example of how one may adapt a recipe taken from a first-rate if high-fat cookbook. There was no reason, other than expense, for substituting chicken for sole, but there were good reasons to cut the amount of oil by two-thirds, and make that half corn oil, instead of all olive oil. I also doubled the lemon juice, making it possible to omit the salt, and replaced half the mayonnaise with yogurt. I also dispensed with the hard-cooked eggs used as decoration in the original recipe: cherry tomatoes and watercress make colorful substitutes.

5 cups cut-up chicken pieces	1 tablespoon olive oil
4 tablespoons chopped shallots	4 tablespoons lemon juice
	¼ teaspoon cayenne pepper
6 tablespoons chopped fresh dill	1 cup mayonnaise
	1 cup skim-milk yogurt
1 tablespoon corn oil	4 tablespoons capers

In food processor, chop the shallots and measure out the approximate amount. Chop the fresh dill with a sharp knife and set half of it aside for the final dressing.

Place shallots and half the dill in a good-sized bowl with oil, lemon juice, and cayenne pepper. Put the cut-up chicken pieces into this mixture and stir until every piece is coated. Marinate this for 1 hour in the refrigerator.

Blend together the mayonnaise and yogurt. Use 1 cup of this to stir into the marinated chicken, and heap this mixture on a platter. Then mix the remaining dill into the remaining cup of mayonnaise and yogurt and slather this over the top of the mound of chicken. Sprinkle capers over all. If you like, surround with cherry tomatoes and sprigs of watercress.

COLD CHICKEN IN TAMARI SAUCE
(Serves 8)

This cold chicken dish is wonderful for a party. It can be easily made ahead of time. If possible, poach two chickens the day before (page 151) so you have almost nothing to do the day of the dinner. With it you might want to have bulgur (page 90) and some baked stuffed tomatoes (page 140). For dessert: prune soufflé (page 197).

5 cups cut-up poached chicken	1 teaspoon honey
4 scallions	1 teaspoon lemon or lime juice
3 cloves garlic	3 tablespoons Tamari sauce
1-inch piece gingerroot, peeled	2 tablespoons chopped parsley
2 tablespoons safflower oil	

With a sharp knife, slice the scallions using both white and green parts. Mix these in a big bowl with the chicken pieces. Peel garlic and gingerroot and chop these in the food processor.

Heat oil in nonstick pan and sauté ginger and garlic lightly. Mix in honey, lemon or lime juice, Tamari sauce, and parsley. Pour this sauce over chicken and scallions and mix well. Marinate this for a few hours in the refrigerator, but be sure you remove the bowl from the refrigerator an hour before you plan to serve the chicken so it is at its savory best.

CURRIED CHICKEN
(Serves 6)

Curried chicken is another very good dish that can be prepared ahead of time so the cook is free to enjoy the evening. For this curry, as for other chicken dishes designed for a party, it's a good idea to poach two chickens the day before (see page 151). It's especially important here because the stock is needed, and it must be chilled overnight so that it can be defatted in the morning.

Serve with a huge bowl of rice, another big bowl of yogurt and cucumbers (page 132), and some warm pita bread. Place the various condiments in small bowls in the center of the table so that people can serve themselves. A green salad is an effective follow-up, and icy beer is a good drink.

4 cups cut-up chicken pieces*	3 tablespoons flour
3 cups chicken stock	3 tablespoons Madras curry powder
3 onions	1 teaspoon tomato paste
1 garlic clove, minced	1 tablespoons orange marmalade
2 stalks celery, with leaves	1 teaspoon lemon juice
1 apple, quartered and seeded	pepper
3 tablespoons corn oil	

Condiments

raisins soaked in Madeira	toasted almonds, slivered
chopped scallions	(page 41)

In food processor, thinly slice onions, garlic, celery, and the apple. Sauté these lightly in oil in a large pot, preferably an enamel-lined iron one.

Heat up the chicken stock in a saucepan.

Mix together flour and curry powder. Sprinkle this over the mixture in the pot and stir it in until the vegetables are completely covered. Cook for 3 minutes. Add tomato paste and the warm stock, and when sauce is well integrated, cover the pot and let it simmer for 20 minutes.

If you are planning to reheat the sauce later, set the pot aside. Reheating should take 10 minutes or so, and when the sauce is hot, add the chicken, pepper, marmalade, and lemon juice. Let the meat cook only long enough to heat through, and then serve the curry immediately.

* Turkey could be used instead of chicken in this dish.

ROAST TURKEY

This marvelous bird is seldom seen during the year, appearing only on the winter holidays when some long-suffering cook has been standing over the stove for hours basting it at regular intervals. This is a waste because turkey is a wonderful way to feed a crowd year-around — a roast turkey can take you through a summer weekend with lots of houseguests — and the basting is not only unnecessary but actually harmful: returning the unwanted grease to its source.

The trick is to cook the turkey upside down, on a rack. The internal juices then flow into the breast, keeping it juicy and moist. It is only cooked breast-side-up for the last half hour or so, in order to brown the skin. You never baste it at all.

Try to get a fresh turkey. If only frozen is available, then avoid the self-basting kind, as they have been injected (yes!) with additional fat.

A 10-pound turkey is a good size. It will feed 10 people amply. Unstuffed it will need 2½ hours of cooking; stuffed, ½ hour longer. These times are, of course, approximate, depending on stoves, altitudes, and other mysterious factors such as the age of the turkey.

Preheat the oven to 450°. Pull off the big chunks of fat just inside the stomach cavity. Rub the turkey all over, inside and out, with a cut lemon. Except at the holiday season, you will probably want to roast the turkey unstuffed: a couple of peeled, halved onions and a handful of fresh herbs are sufficient. For holidays, chestnut stuffing is superb (see page 162).

Sear the turkey at 450° for 20 minutes, then reduce the temperature to 300°. Roast the turkey for 1½ or 2 hours. At this point, remove the turkey with its rack and empty the roasting pan of fat. Return the turkey to the pan, with its breast side up. Pour over it a cup of warmed white wine. Turn up the heat to 350° and roast it for another ½ hour or so, by which time the skin should be browned and beautiful, the meat delicate and juicy. (Prick the flesh with a fork to ascertain doneness; if the fluid comes out colorless, the bird is cooked.)

Let it rest for ½ hour before carving.

CHESTNUT STUFFING

Chestnut stuffing is so rich-tasting it seems orgiastic. And yet, as mentioned earlier, chestnuts are completely fat-free.

1½ pounds chestnuts	1 tablespoon dried mar-
6 cups water	joram
1 onion	pepper
parsley	salt, if desired
2 tablespoons corn or saf-	¾ cup soft bread crumbs*
flower oil	¼ cup milk
1 tablespoon dried thyme	⅓ cup brandy

Boil the chestnuts in water for 20 minutes. While they are still hot, strip them of both inner and outer coverings. Purée them in food processor and then empty container into a bowl; without washing container, use it again to chop the onion and parsley. Sauté these in the oil in a nonstick pan, together with the thyme, marjoram, and pepper. Add the blended chestnuts and taste to see if salt is needed.

Soak bread crumbs in the milk, and then transfer them to the corner of a clean dish towel and squeeze out all the moisture. Add these, with brandy, to the chestnut mixture and stir everything together. Stuff the turkey just before roasting, and close the gap with skewers or coarse thread.

* Toss 3 slices of thin-sliced bread into the blender to achieve instant bread crumbs.

CRANBERRY AND ORANGE RELISH

Make this relish to accompany the chestnut-stuffed holiday bird:

1 bag fresh cranberries
1 whole navel orange
½ cup sugar

2 tablespoons orange
liqueur

Wash cranberries and orange. Cut unpeeled orange into eighths and mix with sugar. In two stages, chop these together in food processor. Add liqueur and chill.

Fish

Unlike chicken, fish is elusive and, once caught, very perishable. Because of this, most fish regrettably is frozen by commercial fishermen. Once this has happened, most of the delicate flavor is lost.

Fresh fish is a prize and so it comes at a price. If you live near a source of fresh fish, get to know your local fish seller. Once it is established that you care intensely about the freshness of the fish, rather than about the specific kind of fish, he or she will probably be frank in telling you which fish just came in. (Avoid fish sellers who are given to sweeping generalizations such as "all our fish are fresh," which is impossible.)

Fresh fish are firm and shiny and their eyes bulge. Since fileted fish lack this final feature, you will have to go by the first two criteria. It is also true that very fresh fish have no smell.

Expensive fish such as salmon, swordfish, and certain kinds of sole are all wonderful-tasting, easy to cook, and easy to love. But the trick, it seems to me, is to make the more modest breeds of fish so tasty that no one recognizes their humble backgrounds. It's far better to have scrod, caught the same day you eat it, than swordfish that either has been frozen or has lain around the store for a matter of days.

Equal in importance to freshness is the manner in which fish is cooked. Less is more: when it is undercooked, fish retains its texture and its flavor. We've been learning from the Japanese, who often don't cook their fish at all. Sushi and sashimi, popular dishes using raw fish, are becoming American favorites.

I prefer fish that is baked briefly at a very high temperature. Covered with a variety of marinades or other toppings, thin filets of sole — baked in a preheated 500° oven — are ready in 3 minutes. Thick filets take as much as 5 minutes to be perfectly cooked.

Steaming fish, another high-heat method, seems to me to have two built-in disadvantages. First, it's hard to move the fish in and out of a steamer without having it fall apart. Second, steamed fish must be seasoned and sauced after cooking. With high-heat baking, you do this work first, and serve the fish from its baking dish.

Another fast way to cook fish is in a stew, in which the fish are steamed with vegetables for no more than 5 minutes. Two ideas for stews are presented here, flavored with my favorite herbs for fish: one is fish stew with dill, the other is fish stew with fennel (pages 172–173).

FILETS OF FISH
WITH GREEN PEPPERCORNS
(Serves 4)

Arrange 4 filets of fish, thick or thin (therefore weighing somewhere between 1 and 1½ pounds) in a baking dish that has been lightly filmed with oil. Cover the filets with

juice of 1 lemon
1 shallot, minced
6 whole green peppercorns, crushed

chopped fresh tarragon (or oregano or some other herb)

In a preheated 500° oven, bake this fish for 3 minutes if you're having filet of sole, or 5 minutes if you're having one of the thick filets.

FISH FILETS WITH ANCHOVIES
(Serves 6)

For 6 people, 2 to 2½ pounds of fish filets is appropriate on a low-fat diet where you always serve supporting foods, such as rice, bulgur, or tiny new potatoes.

An anchovy sauce makes for an exciting contrast to one of the thick filets of either scrod, haddock, halibut, red snapper, or whatever is freshest in your fish store.

The following sauce is recommended for anyone not on a low-salt diet.

1 tin flat anchovies, drained	2 tablespoons lemon juice
2 cloves garlic	handful fresh, chopped
2 tablespoons capers	parsley
2 tablespoons Tamari sauce	

Mince garlic and add it to the food processor with capers and anchovies, whirling until you have a smooth paste. Add Tamari, parsley, and lemon juice. Spread this mixture over fish in a lightly oiled baking dish and bake for 5 minutes or so in a preheated, 500° oven.

SWORDFISH CHUNKS
(Serves 4)

Sometimes one can find chunk pieces of swordfish, along with cod's tongues and cheeks — both great bargains — at a fish market; 1½ pounds of either will make a delightful dish for 4 people. When marinated in the following Asian-inspired sauce, they need almost no cooking.

1 clove garlic	Szechuan pepper
1 onion	2 tablespoons Tamari sauce
½-inch piece of gingerroot	1 tablespoon lemon juice
generous amount of	few drops sesame oil
chopped parsley	

In food processor, chop the garlic, onion, ginger, and parsley together. Cut the fish into bite-sized pieces. Place all these in a bowl with seasonings and marinate in the refrigerator for an hour.

Drain the marinade, and sauté the fish for 1 or 2 minutes on each side, in a well-heated nonstick pan onto which you have sprinkled a few drops of sesame oil. Serve immediately.

FILETS OF SOLE
STUFFED WITH SCALLOPS
(Serves 6)

This is a marvelous dish that can be prepared ahead of time, then kept refrigerated until ½ hour before you cook it.

6 slices filet of sole (2½ pounds)	1 tablespoon parsley
	⅓ pound scallops
2 shallots	black pepper
1 tablespoon fresh dill or tarragon	¼ cup white wine
	2 tablespoons lemon juice

In food processor, chop the shallots and fresh herbs. With a sharp knife, thinly slice the scallops. Place these ingredients in a small bowl, sprinkle with pepper, and moisten with some of the white wine.

Lay the filets out on the kitchen counter and place a small amount of stuffing in the center of each slice. Roll up each filet and place it neatly in a shallow baking dish. Squeeze lemon juice over the filets, and add enough white wine to the dish to cover the bottom.

Preheat the oven to 500°, and then bake the sole for 10 minutes.

FILETS OF SOLE
IN ASPIC
(Serves 6)

I like to serve small dinners with a number of courses, and this dish is a perfect first course. Admittedly, all aspics are more work than other dishes, but their elegance and delicate taste (as well as the fact that they must be prepared ahead of time) seem to justify their inclusion in this book.

For a second course, you might have pasta. This could be followed by either cold artichokes or cold asparagus, depending on the season.

Make this dish when you have some fish stock on hand (page 65) or use the recipe to inspire you to make the stock from scratch (using free bones from the fish store).

First, cook the filets.

6 filets of sole (2 pounds)	**1 tablespoon lemon juice**
1 tablespoon rice wine vinegar	**pepper**

Preheat oven to 500°. Place fish in a single layer on a lightly oiled baking dish and pour vinegar and lemon juice over them. Sprinkle on the pepper, and bake fish for 3 minutes. Remove from oven.

Prepare the aspic:

1 cup fish stock	**½ package gelatin**
½ cup white wine	**2 tablespoons cold water**
minced parsley	
fresh thyme leaves (or another fresh herb)	

Over high heat, boil the stock and wine together with the parsley and thyme leaves until the liquid is reduced to less than 1 cup. (This should take only a few minutes.)

Mix the gelatin with the cold water, and when this is thick, mix it into the warm stock and pour it over the fish. Chill the fish for 2 hours or so, by which time the stock should be jelled.

FISH STEW WITH DILL
(Serves 6)

This stew is so handsome and so tasty that it appears to be something of a production. Nothing could be less true: it's as simple as can be, and takes about 20 minutes to cook. First, buy 18 mussels and 2½ pounds of fish: haddock, halibut, scrod, or tongues and cheeks of cod — any of these would do fine.

Serve tiny steamed potatoes with this stew.

18 mussels	6-8 Italian plum tomatoes
2½ pounds of fish filets	(fresh or canned)
3 onions	1 cup white wine
4 cloves garlic	handful of fresh, chopped
1 tablespoon corn or saf-	dill
flower oil	cayenne pepper

First, scrub the mussels thoroughly, and, on this occasion, since the mussels are cooked in the stew, cut off beards and barnacles. Soak them in cold water until ready to cook.

In food processor, thinly slice the onions and garlic.

In a large pot (preferably enamel lined), place the oil, onions, garlic, tomatoes, and wine.* Cover the pot and steam gently for 15 minutes or so, until vegetables are tender.

While they are stewing, cut the fish into chunks. Add these to the pot, together with the mussels, and cook for 5 minutes more — when the mussels should be open. Finally, throw in a handful of dill, add a little cayenne pepper, and serve it forth.

* Should you happen to have any homemade lobster stock in the freezer, add ½ cup of it with the wine to this stew; it's a heavenly addition. See page 63 for easy production of lobster stock.

FISH STEW WITH FENNEL
(Serves 8)

This is a marvelous stew, which can be made with the most ordinary fish — cod, for example, perhaps in combination with monkfish, which has a lobsterlike texture. It's best with fresh fennel, but fennel seeds alone will give a good anise flavor in any case. Serve this stew in bowls with hot, fresh French or Italian bread.

3 pounds fish	2 cups white wine
1 tablespoon corn or saf-flower oil	1 bay leaf
2 thick slices fresh fennel (or 2 stalks celery)	crushed red pepper (or cayenne)
2 potatoes, peeled and quartered	2 strips orange peel
	thyme, fresh or dried
3 cloves garlic	1 teaspoon fennel seeds
3 large shallots	pinch of sugar
1 28-ounce can plum tomatoes, drained	dash of salt
	½ cup chopped parsley

In food processor, thinly slice fennel or celery, potatoes, garlic, and shallots. Stir these in hot oil in an enamel-lined pot. Add tomatoes, wine, and all seasonings except parsley, and let this simmer, covered, for ½ hour or so.

Just before serving, cut fish into chunks and add these to pot. Cover pot and let it simmer for no more than 5 minutes. Add ½ cup chopped parsley and serve immediately.

Shellfish

Shellfish abound on the coasts of this country, and in New England, clams, lobsters, mussels, and sea scallops are summertime regulars. Oysters and bay scallops are fall and winter specialties.

The only major shellfish not found in the Northeast is shrimp, which needs to be frozen and imported from the Gulf of Mexico. But since it's very high in cholesterol, as well as in price, you may find that you can do without it quite easily.

Lobster is the prize, best in Maine. But heavenly mussels are still regarded as so lowly that they remain unprotected by local authorities. You don't need a license to gather them, so if you are lucky enough to find a cache of them, take all you want. We've found several beds in the tidal marsh near our house, and I guess that explains the unusual emphasis given to mussels in this book.

Even if you don't live near a mussel bed, don't worry: most fish stores now carry them. You'll find them to be the cheapest of all the shellfish, and once they are well seasoned, as delicious as any.

HARD-SHELL CLAMS

Littlenecks and cherrystones are the two smallest and tenderest of these clams. They should be eaten raw, served immediately after opening, with a cut half lemon provided with each plateful.

What a treat this is, ennobling special occasions such as New Year's Eve or an important birthday. However, the job of opening clams (or oysters) is awesome. Once you get the hang of it, it can go fairly quickly, but acquiring experience may be a little arduous. In any event, should you decide to do this, you will need a lesson from a practiced expert. Then, a clam knife and a pair of very thick gloves will assure you of safety as well as success.

Larger clams are called quahogs (or chowder clams), the largest of which are sea clams (whose shells used to be used in summer houses for ashtrays). Quahogs can be opened by steaming them briefly using ½ cup of water in a large pot. The clam meat may then be chopped in the food processor, and is then ready to use in spaghetti sauce (page 104). The abundant clam broth that issues forth from steaming clams can be frozen and served later — perhaps combined with chicken broth, to make a superb clear soup.

STEAMED CLAMS

Oval-shaped, soft-shell clams — "steamers" — need to be washed thoroughly in several waters so you can be sure they are entirely free of sand.

Heat ½ cup of water in the bottom of a large pot. When water bubbles, add clams, cover, and steam them until they open — 5 minutes or so.

There will be a lot of clam broth. Strain into a bowl, and then ladle it out into individual cups, perhaps giving a squirt of lemon juice to each.

Serve the clams from a large tureen. Eat them with your fingers. They need no butter to be absolutely delicious.

STEAMED LOBSTER

Individual steamed lobsters are an exciting dish to serve at a feast — to celebrate Christmas, or the beginning of summer. This stunning meal, accomplished with very little work, will cost much less at home than an ordinary meal costs in even a modest restaurant.

Buy lobsters weighing 1¼ pounds apiece. Steam them in a huge pot, in 4 inches of rapidly boiling water. Put each lobster into the pot head down, and cover the pot briefly until the water boils again: then add the next lobster.

Serve the lobsters without butter or lemon juice: they will taste exquisitely of themselves. Follow them with an enormous green salad and toasted French bread. For dessert, the justly famous ricotta dish (page 200). Icy champagne would be the perfect drink.

Don't throw out the lobster shells. Refrigerate or freeze them until you have time to cook them. Put them into a pot with 4–6 cups of cold water (best of all would be their original steaming water). Boil the shells uncovered until liquid is reduced to 1 or 2 cups. Strain this stock and freeze it in small containers, carefully labeled; use it in fish stew with dill (page 172) or other dishes.

LOBSTER SALAD
(Serves 6)

Less expensive than individual lobsters, a lobster salad is a terrific treat. Have it at a summer lunch or supper when you're feeling particularly good.

3 cups cooked lobster meat	1 tablespoon lemon juice
2 tablespoons oil (corn oil)	cayenne pepper

Buy a lively 3-pound lobster and steam it in boiling water for 18 minutes. Cool it quickly in running water, and cut it up. (Don't throw out the lobster shells! See instructions above for making stock.) There should be about 3 cups of lobster meat. Marinate this in the refrigerator for 1 hour in oil, lemon juice, and a little cayenne pepper.

Remove it from the refrigerator and make a sauce:

1 cup mayonnaise	fresh lettuce leaves (or
1 cup sliced celery	cherry tomatoes and
2 tablespoons fresh tarragon	sprigs of parsley)
2 tablespoons capers	

Slice celery, using a sharp knife, into inch-long slivers. Blend this with ½ cup mayonnaise. Stir the fresh tarragon leaves into the other ½ cup mayonnaise.

Combine the lobster with the celery-mayonnaise mixture and arrange this in a mound on a platter. Slather over the top the tarragon mayonnaise. Sprinkle capers over all. Surround with fresh lettuce leaves, or a few cherry tomatoes and sprigs of parsley.

STEAMED MUSSELS

For much of the year, we live near a tidal marsh, where there is a big mussel bed so remote from the world that the mussel population multiplies from year to year. It's satisfying to find free food, and I even quite enjoy the necessary cleaning and scrubbing. I turn up the stereo and go with the flow.

Mussels need to be washed in several waters and, if possible, to soak in clean cold water for an hour to get rid of any lingering suggestion of mud or sand. I have learned to ignore any barnacles clinging to the shells, and no longer do I chop off the occasional "beard." They all disappear into the stock during the steaming process, and are easily strained out.

In a fish store, good fresh mussels are tightly closed. Allow about 2 pounds per person (approximately 24). Since mussels don't have the staying power of clams, eat them as soon after getting them as possible.

In the bottom of a large pot, place everything but the chopped parsley — an unvarying quantity whether you're cooking 4 or 12 pounds of mussels:

½ cup dry vermouth
4 chopped shallots
1 minced garlic clove
fresh sprigs of thyme and
    parsley

black pepper
handful of chopped parsley
    for garnish

Bring this mixture to a bubbling boil. Add the mussels, cover the pot, and steam until they open. This might take anywhere from 5 to 20 minutes, depending on the number of mussels. Stir the mussels once or twice, if you're cooking a lot, to encourage them to all cook at approximately the same speed.

Ladle the mussels into a big bowl or soup tureen. Pour the sauce through a strainer over the mussels and, finally, toss a handful of parsley over all. Use the mussel shells as spoons. Save the extra stock to use as a medium for cooking rice.

MUSSELS AND SCALLOPS WITH RICE
(Serves 6)

This dish is an ideal way of using up leftovers. You may have both mussels and rice left over, in which case all you need do is buy a pound of scallops. Slice these and simmer them for 2 minutes in some of the mussel broth. Add the cooked mussels but barely heat them. If you have no rice left over, then by all means cook 1 cup rice with 2 cups mussel broth (see above). When everything is hot, make a little sauce.

1 teaspoon safflower oil
2 minced shallots (or 2
    minced garlic cloves)

½ cup (or more) vermouth
minced parsley

Heat shallots (or garlic) in the warm oil. Add wine and bring to boil. Stir this into the hot rice and shellfish mixture and sprinkle parsley over all.

OYSTERS

Oysters are a delicacy, when eaten raw, like clams (page 177). Best with only a lashing of lemon juice for sauce.

SCALLOPS

There are three kinds of scallops that we feast on throughout the year in the Northeast. Sea scallops, native to our waters year-round, are the largest and they are excellent.

Small, bay scallops come from the waters around Long Island during the winter. Shucked by hand, they are expensive, but as they are particularly tender and sweet many people don't find this an obstacle.

In recent years, calicos, small scallops harvested in the waters off Florida and the Carolinas, have become available. They are much cheaper than other scallops since they are harvested and shucked mechanically. They are flown north on a daily basis, and if you can find some, consider yourself fortunate.

Scallops need only the briefest cooking; overdone, they become rubbery. Whole or sliced, they can be quickly sautéed or broiled, then seasoned with lemon juice and pepper.

Alternatively, scallops may be combined with minced shallots, pepper, and a handful of chopped dill. Covered with white wine and lemon juice, they may be heated up in a 500° oven for 3 minutes. After this, they are delicious eaten by themselves, or they may be tossed into a bowl of fresh hot pasta or rice.

COLD SCALLOPS
(Serves 8)

Seviche is the name of the dish in which scallops marinated in lime juice may be served cold. It makes an elegant hors d'oeuvre or first course for a very grand dinner.

3 pounds small scallops   1 tiny piece hot green chili
2 cups fresh lime juice   pepper
1 small white onion or   minced parsley or dill
    scallion, chopped   pepper

Marinate the raw scallops in the lime juice in the refrigerator for 12 to 24 hours. Before serving (with melba toast for hors d'oeuvres, or in small dishes at the table), drain them of most of their juice, add herbs, vegetables, and sprinkle with pepper.

Fruits and Desserts

"What's for dessert?" is still a good question, and even though we are pleased with fresh fruit and yogurt most of the time, we usually have a special dessert when we have guests for dinner. Most of the desserts are based on fruit: cut up and laced with marmalade or liqueur, poached in wine, or combined with whipped egg whites into soufflés. Other desserts combine ricotta with yogurt, and still others are drawn from childhood: Indian pudding and snow pudding. Meringues and macaroons are sugary blessings, made without an ounce of fat.

But fresh fruit itself is a wonderful dessert, and since it varies from one season to the next we don't weary of any one kind. Summer is, of course, prime time, with cherries, rhubarb, watermelon, peaches, plums, nectarines, and all the berries. In fall, apples, grapes, and pears tumble off the trees and vines. By winter, oranges and grapefruit begin coming up from Florida in abundance, and clementines, tangerines, and kumquats are available beginning in December.

There are year-round fruits, too, and it's nice to mix these with the seasonal ones. A combination of chilled fruits, such as peaches, bananas, and strawberries, emerge from the blender as a cold, creamy-textured dessert, a wonderful substitute for ice cream. Bananas are indispensable. California navel oranges are essential to have on hand at all times; their flesh and peelings make superb desserts. Mangoes and papayas are also to be found year-round now, imported from the tropics, and they, together with kiwis, are small luxuries well worth the price.

APPLE CRISP
(Serves 8)

This is a wonderful dessert in fall, when the apples are newly picked. Cortlands are good in this dish, but any fresh, firm apple will do.

8 apples, unpeeled, quartered and seeded	2 tablespoons orange juice
juice and rind of 1 lemon	½ cup cider or water

Grate the peel of a lemon, and then squeeze it for its juice. In food processor, slice the apples thickly, and place them in a baking dish. Pour the fruit juices over them. Stir in the lemon rind and cider or water.

Topping

2 tablespoons margarine	1 teaspoon cinnamon
¼ cup walnuts	1 teaspoon coriander
½ cup brown sugar (page 25)	½ teaspoon fresh-ground nutmeg
1 cup bread crumbs (use 3 slices bread; page 25)	¼ teaspoon clove

Prepare the brown sugar and bread crumbs by the simple methods described on page 25.

Chop the walnuts coarsely with a sharp knife.

In nonstick pan, melt the margarine, add the other ingredients, and mix well. Spread this crumbly mixture over the apples in the baking dish, leaving no open spaces.

When you sit down for dinner, put the apple crisp into a 350° oven for 20 to 30 minutes. Serve with a topping made of ricotta cheese and yogurt (see page 54).

APPLESAUCE

The good news is that, with a food processor, applesauce no longer needs to be cooked. The apples don't even need to be peeled, just quartered and seeded. The taste is special.

Wash 4 large, firm apples (use 2 McIntosh and 2 Cortlands for interesting flavor). Cut them into quarters and brush off the seeds. Drop these pieces into the food processor, together with ½ lemon that has also been washed and cut into pieces. Turn the machine on and off at first, until the apples become a smooth, juicy mixture. Then leave the machine on for a minute or two.

Depending on the freshness of the apples, serve the applesauce as it is, warm or cold, or seasoned with some ground coriander, nutmeg, and a scoop of fresh yogurt.

APRICOT FLUFF
(*Serves 6*)

This glorious dessert needs about 3 hours to chill.

1 cup dried apricots	2 tablespoons lemon juice
2 cups water	3 tablespoons brandy
½ cup honey	4 egg whites

In a saucepan, cover apricots with the water, bring to a boil, and simmer gently for 15 minutes or so, until apricots are soft. Put them in the food processor with 4 tablespoons of their cooking liquid, plus the honey, lemon juice, and brandy. Whirl them well and then cool them in a large bowl.

Beat the egg whites until stiff and gently fold into the apricot mixture. Chill.

Ricotta and yogurt sauce is perfect as topping for this dish, as well as several others. (See page 54.)

BANANAS

Hearty, healthful, delicious, and available year-round, bananas (rich in potassium) are said to relieve existential despair. I believe it. They adapt beautifully to other fruits and to yogurt. If you are out on the town and don't want to take time to stop to eat, a banana makes a robust lunch by itself.

BANANAS WITH GRAPEFRUIT
(Serves 6)

During the winter, we have this dessert constantly and never seem to get tired of it.

3 bananas	2 tablespoons marmalade:
3 grapefruit	ginger, grapefruit, or-
1–2 kiwis	ange, or lemon*

Slice bananas and kiwis, and cut out grapefruit sections with a fruit knife. Squeeze the rinds for all their juice and put about ½ cup of it into a small bowl as the base for a sauce for the fruit. Mix into this a generous dollop of marmalade, and pour over the fruit. Chill.

BAKED BANANAS
(Serves 4)

Lightly oil a shallow baking dish and place in it 4 bananas, halved lengthwise. Over these, pour some lemon juice and honey. Sprinkle on some cinnamon, nutmeg, and powdered ginger. Top with a tablespoon or two of Kirsch or maple syrup. Bake in a moderate oven (325°) for 15 minutes.

BANANA FREEZE
(Serves 4)

This astonishing concoction tastes like very rich ice cream. It's hard to believe it's made only of fruit.

Slice 4 bananas, and put them in a plastic container suitable for the freezer. Sprinkle a tablespoon or 2 of lemon juice over them and mix it in well. Freeze.

To make the dessert, drop the frozen slices of banana into the food processor, a few at a time. Keep churning them until the consistency is that of ice cream. Best eaten right away, this can also be stored in the freezer for a day or two. (It crystallizes if you leave it longer and needs rewhipping.)

BANANA IN YOGURT

This is a perfect diet lunch, a meal in itself. Cut a banana in pieces and add a little yogurt before whirling it, on and off, in the blender. When it's well mixed, add 1 cup more yogurt and mix briefly (since yogurt liquefies so quickly). Drink it from a glass. Luscious.

BRANDIED DRIED FRUITS

This preserved fruit is excellent as a topping on cut-up bananas, oranges, and grapefruit in the late winter. It's also a fine addition to plain ricotta. It improves in flavor with time, so once you've made it, let the mixture rest for as long as you can restrain yourself.

1½ cups dried apricots, pears, prunes, raisins, or other fruits	1 tablespoon honey ¾ cup (or more) brandy

Cover dried fruit with boiling water and let stand for 5 minutes. Drain. Trickle honey over the fruit and mix in. Fill clear glass jars ⅞ full of this fruit. Top off each jar with brandy (cheap brandy will do fine) and seal them tight. These fruits, in attractive jars, could make fine Christmas presents.

An excellent sauce for meringues (page 193), especially in wintertime, is made of 8 oranges, crushed in the food processor, combined with 1 cup (or more) of these brandied fruits.

INDIAN PUDDING
(*Serves 6*)

This appears to be a delicate dessert, in both flavor and texture, but it's actually very sturdy. Serve it hot, after a meal that has not included any grain dishes.

4 cups skim milk	½ teaspoon salt
½ cup yellow cornmeal	½ teaspoon ground ginger
1 teaspoon margarine	1 whole egg plus 1 egg
½ cup dark molasses	white*
1 teaspoon cinnamon	

Mix the cornmeal with 1 cup of the cold milk. Scald the other 3 cups of milk in a double boiler until bubbles begin appearing around the edge. Then, slowly add the cornmeal and keep stirring it with a wire whisk until it is completely blended and the mixture has thickened. Be sure there are no lumps. Cover the pot and cook for 20 minutes.

Add all the other ingredients to this mixture except for the eggs. Mix well and cool.

In a large bowl, beat the eggs (not too vigorously) and add them to the cornmeal. Pour mixture into a greased soufflé dish. Preheat oven to 350°. Put an inch of water into the bottom of a roasting pan in the oven and place soufflé dish in the pan. Bake 1 hour and serve immediately.

* If you are in a stage in life when you don't want even a single egg yolk to contaminate one of your dishes, then make this pudding with two egg whites and chill it so it becomes properly firm, then serve it cold. Incidentally, the original recipe calls for three whole eggs. I think that when you make this dessert as described here, you'll be glad not to have all that extra heaviness.

MACAROONS
(Makes about 28)

Made of almond paste, which is sold in rolls in a number of supermarkets as well as specialty shops, macaroons are a delectable treat in an otherwise no-cookie diet.

| 8 ounces almond paste | ⅞ cup sugar |
| 2 egg whites | a few grains of salt |

Cut the almond paste up into smallish pieces and place it with sugar and 1 egg white in the food processor. Turn machine on and off to get the mixture free of lumps. Then add the other egg white and whirl until you have a perfectly smooth paste.

Preheat oven to 325°. Cover baking sheets with foil. Using a teaspoon, drop macaroon paste onto the sheets, allowing space for the macaroons to spread out. Bake them for 25 to 30 minutes. Immediately, remove foil from baking sheets and let them cool on the kitchen counter. As soon as macaroons are crisp enough to move, scoop them off the foil with fingers or a spatula, and arrange them on a large platter. They disappear so fast you may have a hard time getting one.

MANGOES

The mango is a tropical blessing, but it is not easy to work with. Its stone is tremendous and the luscious flesh adheres firmly to it. However, cut the fruit off the stone as best you can, eating as you go, or combine it with other fruits in a bowl.

MERINGUES WITH FRUIT
(*Serves 12*)

My recipe for meringues is no different from any other. I include it only in order to show how luxurious a low-fat diet can be.

6 egg whites	1½ cups fine white sugar
¼ teaspoon salt	1 teaspoon vanilla extract
¼ teaspoon cream of tartar	

Beat egg whites with salt and cream of tartar until they are stiff, but not dry. Add the sugar in tiny amounts, beating until it is well absorbed. Continue beating, after sugar is used up, until mixture is glossy. Add vanilla and blend it in well.

In preheated 225° oven, place teaspoonfuls of meringue about an inch apart on a baking sheet covered with wax paper or foil. Bake for about 50 minutes until they are palest beige. After taking from oven, remove the meringues from the wax paper or foil as soon as they are cool enough to handle. Gently place them on large platter; they are terribly fragile.

Serve with crushed strawberries, raspberries, peaches, or the brandied fruit sauce described on page 191.

CANDIED ORANGE PEEL

In winter, when California navel oranges are abundant, buy 8 of them and make candied orange peel. This peel is a marvelous addition to sliced oranges and other fruits, and it is also good on yogurt, in demitasse, and to use as a snack during the holidays. Candied peel takes only minutes to make, but it keeps well for weeks if you take some pains to hide the jar.

Using a vegetable peeler, pare off the orange skins, leaving the white pulp on the oranges as intact as possible. Simmer peel in boiling water for 10 minutes, drain, and chop in food processor. Measure out an equal amount of sugar, and combine sugar and peels in an iron frying pan.* Cook, stirring constantly, for a few minutes over moderate heat, until moisture is first absorbed and then released. Keep stirring until the peels are quite crisp and dry. Spread on board to cool, then store in a glass jar.

* After being used a few times for peels, this pan should be wiped with oil and "seasoned" in a slow oven for an hour to revitalize its surface.

CANDIED ORANGE PEEL AND SLICED ORANGES
(Serves 8)

Scrape all the white pulp from the outside of 8 oranges, and take out any white pulp at the core. Slice the oranges crosswise, or separate them into segments. Squeeze 1 or 2 Florida juice oranges over the fruit and add a little orange liqueur. Chill. Just before serving, sprinkle candied orange peel over the top. A lovely dessert.

ORANGE SHERBET
IN FROZEN SHELLS
(*Serves 8*)

This is a handsome dessert, which might be further enhanced by a tiny mint leaf on top of each orange. These sherbet-filled oranges need 24 hours of freezing time to be at their best.

8 handsome Indian River oranges
8 tablespoons orange sherbet
1 teaspoon almond extract

Cut off the top third of each orange. Grate the rind from these tops, and squeeze their juice into a large bowl.

Using a fruit knife and a tablespoon, scoop out the flesh of the oranges. After removing any offending pulp, whirl the orange flesh in the food processor. If the orange shells contain any extra juice, empty this into a pitcher.

Add 8 heaping tablespoons of sherbet to the juice in the large bowl. Stir in the crushed oranges and the grated orange rind, together with the almond extract. If mixture needs more moisture, add a little of the fresh orange juice.

Pack each orange shell to the brim with the sherbet and orange filling. Fit the oranges into a shallow container (two ice trays would be suitable) and place them in the freezer. Freeze them for 24 hours, and bring them forth about 10 minutes before you serve them.

PAPAYAS

The papaya is a succulent treasure, and whenever you find a ripe yellow one, consider yourself fortunate. Preparation is simple: cut the chilled fruit in half, excise all the black seeds, and fill the cavity with a mixture of fresh lime juice and a dash of crème de cassis. A stalk of fresh mint is a nice summertime touch.

PEACHES IN RED WINE

When your palate has been satiated by fresh peaches in summertime, you might on occasion want to make a fancy dessert out of them. With very little trouble, I might add.

Peel the peaches with a sharp knife. Or, if you prefer, pour some boiling water over them, wait 10 seconds, and then pull the skin off in large strips.

Slice peaches into a big bowl or individual goblets. Sprinkle them with sugar and a variety of spices: cardamom, coriander, cloves, cinnamon, and/or nutmeg are all appropriate. Cover with red wine and chill.

POACHED PEARS IN RED WINE
(*Serves 8*)

This fine party dessert needs to be made ahead of time and chilled.

8 unpeeled Bosc pears	½ cup water
8 cloves	½ cup sugar
1½ cups red wine	

Insert a clove into each pear and place them in an enamel-lined pot with a cover. Make a syrup of wine, water, and sugar and cook this for a few minutes until sugar is completely dissolved. Pour over the pears. Simmer them, covered, for 30 minutes. Uncover pot, baste the pears, and continue cooking for 15 more minutes. Chill.

Serve European style with knives and forks.

PERSIMMONS

Persimmons are beautiful, and when fully ripened, they make gorgeous eating. They are available mostly in winter. Cut a persimmon in half and eat it by itself. Or, for a superb sauce to pour over ricotta or meringues, purée a couple of persimmons in the food processor, add a little lemon juice, and enjoy. Persimmons are also an excellent addition to salad (see page 147).

PRUNE SOUFFLÉ
(*Serves 6*)

This soufflé is an easy-to-make, light, and delicious dessert.

1 cup pitted prunes*	½ lemon, cut in pieces (rind
½ cup boiling water	and fruit)
½ cup walnuts	5 egg whites
¼ cup sugar	

Place prunes in boiling water in a saucepan and simmer them for 5 minutes. Drain. Grind the walnuts in the food processor. Add prunes, sugar, and lemon, and whirl all together until smooth. Empty container into a large bowl.

Preheat oven to 300°. Heat up a roasting pan, filled to the depth of 1 inch with water.

Beat egg whites until stiff, but not dry. Gently fold them into the prune mixture (or vice versa), trying to incorporate as much air as you can. Fill an ungreased soufflé dish with this, and place dish in the roasting pan. Cook the soufflé for 45 minutes and serve immediately.

* Much valuable time can be saved by buying pitted prunes.

PRUNES WITH KUMQUATS
(*Serves 6*)

Kumquats appear in the market in December and are around until April. I like to have a bowl of them, nestled in their leaves, on the coffee table during the holidays, along with the traditional bowl of unshelled nuts.

Kumquats do something special for prunes.

1 pound pitted prunes	cold water
½ pound kumquats, halved and seeded	stick of cinnamon
	1 teaspoon sugar

Cover prunes, kumquats, and cinnamon stick with cold water. Cook them in a saucepan over medium heat for no more than 5 minutes. Drain fruit, catching juice in another saucepan. Add sugar to the juice and cook, stirring at first, for about 5 minutes. Place fruit in serving dish, pour syrup over all, and chill.

SNOW PUDDING
(Serves 6)

This is an old-time favorite dessert, adapted from an early Fanny Farmer cookbook. She was the genie of American kitchens, before Irma Rombauer came on the scene with *The Joy of Cooking* and exotic notions about paprika and sherry.

As usual, the sugar content in the original recipe was very high, and I cut it in half to good effect. The classic sauce for this pudding was custard, made with egg yolks. I have substituted strawberry sauce, which is more exciting and better-looking.

1 tablespoon gelatin	½ cup sugar
¼ cup cold water	½ cup fresh lemon juice
1 cup boiling water	3 egg whites

Soak gelatin in cold water, then dissolve this mixture in boiling water. Stir in sugar and lemon juice. When sugar is absorbed, pour this mixture into a bowl and chill it for a couple of hours.

Beat the egg whites until stiff, and then, without washing the beaters, whip the gelatin mixture. Gently fold the egg whites into the lemon jelly and chill again. Serve with strawberry sauce:

Strawberry Sauce

1 small box strawberries (fresh or frozen)
1 tablespoon sugar
1 tablespoon orange juice or orange liqueur

Give all ingredients a fast whirl in the blender and a chilling. Pour into a pitcher and serve with snow pudding.

STRAWBERRIES SEVILLE
(Serves 8)

A sauce based on marmalade is particularly suitable for California strawberries, which begin arriving in New York in February. Fresh local strawberries (which on the East Coast appear in June) seem perfect without any sauce (unless, for a special occasion, you cover them with crushed fresh raspberries).

1 quart hulled strawberries	½ cup fresh orange juice
1 cup Seville (bitter) orange marmalade	1 tablespoon candied orange peel (page 194)
3 tablespoons orange liqueur	½ teaspoon lemon juice

Place strawberries in serving bowl. Mix everything else together in another bowl. Pour this mixture over the fruit and stir in well. Chill. Macaroons (page 192) would complete this elegant dessert.

YOGURT AND RICOTTA DESSERTS

Yogurt can always lend a cool and distinctive conclusion to a meal, especially when it is enhanced by a scattering of currants on top, plus some candied orange peel (see page 194) or candied ginger. For a sugar-free topping, use fresh-grated gingerroot.

As we all know, yogurt can also be improved by the addition of jam. I like to use ginger marmalade, and sometimes black currant jam. This latter goes especially well if ricotta and yogurt are combined together in equal amounts and infused with crème de cassis, poured on at the last moment.

Yogurt makes a happy medium for fresh and dried fruit. Try combining seedless green grapes with slices of dried apricot in a bowl of fresh yogurt. One caveat: if you are using some juicy fruit such as peaches, be sure to add the yogurt only at the last minute; otherwise, the dish will become watery.

The best and easiest dessert in this book (mentioned in the Introduction) is ricotta with Kahlua. This is especially desirable if you can get freshly made ricotta, bought in an Italian shop where it's made every day. For a party of 8, set out 8 dessert dishes on the counter and put a dollop of ricotta into each. Top with Kahlua and a scattering of candied orange peel (page 194), or chopped candied ginger. If you have no Kahlua you can substitute brandy. In this case you would need to put 1 teaspoon each of finely ground instant coffee and brown sugar on top of the ricotta, before adding the brandy. This is more trouble but the effect is almost as good.

Index

Index   205

206 Index

Index 207

208 Index

Grilled, on the Cob, 131
Steamed, on the Cob, 130–131
Cucumber(s), 131–133
    as hors d'oeuvre, 42, 131
    Hot, and Green Pepper, 132–133
    in Yogurt, 132
Eggplant, Broiled in Tomato
    Sauce, 133–134
Endive, Belgian, as hors d'oeuvre,
    42
Fennel as hors d'oeuvre, 42
Green Beans, 134–135
    as hors d'oeuvre, 42
    Purée of, 134
    Salad, 135
    juices, 35
Mushrooms, 135–136
    Duxelles, 135–136
    as hors d'oeuvre, 42
    Stuffed, 46–47
    Tree Ear, Chicken with, 154–155
Onion(s)
    and Carrot Purée, 125–126
    Poached White, 136–137
organic, avoiding, 23–24
Peas
    Green, 137
    as hors d'oeuvre, 43
    Puréed, 137
    Snow, 43, 138
Peppers, Green
    as hors d'oeuvre, 42
    Hot Cucumbers and, 132–133
Potatoes, 138
    New, Steamed, 138
Radishes as hors d'oeuvre, 42, 43
    raw, as hors d'oeuvre, 41–43
Scallions as hors d'oeuvre, 42
shopping for, 21–22, 23
Spinach, 139
    with Pine Nuts, 139
Squash, Acorn, 118
Tomatoes, 140–141
    Baked Stuffed, 140–141

Broiled, 141
    as hors d'oeuvre, 42
    Zucchini as hors d'oeuvre, 43
    See also Salads; Soup
Vinaigrette
    Artichokes, 119
    Salad Dressing, 56
Vinegar, 9, 17

Walnut(s), 40
    oil, 19–20, 23
    Sauce, Hot Broccoli with, 122
White
    Bean Soup, Escarole and, 70
    onions. See Onions
    pepper. See Pepper
    wine, 17
Whole grains, 81–82, 90–97
    See also individual kinds
Whole Wheat Bread, 95–97
Wine
    Red
        Peaches in, 196
        Poached Pears in, 196
    white, 17
Wire rack, 27
Worcestershire sauce, 17

Yellow onions. See Onions
Yogurt, 12, 20, 25, 27, 51
    Banana in, 191
    and Cottage Cheese Sauce, 52–54
    Cucumbers in, 132
    for dessert, 199–200
    with fruit, 191, 200
    Mayonnaise, 55–56
    and Ricotta Cheese Sauce, 54
    Skim-Milk, Homemade, 52
Yogurt maker, 27

Ziti with Spinach, 107
Zucchini
    as hors d'oeuvre, 43
    Soup, 77–78